Beef up your revision muscles with CGP!

It's not easy to rack up a high score in GCSE PE — and the new Grade 9-1 course is tougher than ever. Luckily, help is at hand...

This brilliant CGP Revision Guide explains everything you need to know for the OCR exams, from synovial joints to sponsorship! There are also plenty of exam-style questions to test you on what you've learned.

We've also included advice on how to pick up as many marks as possible, so you'll be ready to tackle your exams and finish with style.

CGP — still the best! ☺

Our sole aim here at CGP is to produce the highest quality books — carefully written, immaculately presented and dangerously close to being funny.

Then we work our socks off to get them out to you — at the cheapest possible prices.

Contents

Component 1 — Physical Factors Affecting Performance

Section Four — Socio-Cultural Influences

Section Five — Sport Psychology

Section Six — Health, Fitness and Well-Being

Section Seven — Using Data

Published by CGP

Editors:
Katie Fernandez, Kelsey Hammond, Sharon Keeley-Holden, Camilla Sheridan and Michael Weynberg.

Contributor:
Paddy Gannon

With thanks to Chris Cope and James Summersgill for the proofreading.

With thanks to Jan Greenway for the copyright research.

Definitions from Edexcel specifications used with the permission of Pearson Education.

Normative data table for grip dynamometer test on page 22 was published in 'Physical Education and the Study of Sport' 4th ed, 2002, Davis ed, p.123, 1 table ('Normative data table for grip strength test' for 16 to 19 year olds), Copyright Elsevier (2016).

Graph on page 36 based on data from Sport England.

Definition of health on page 48 is from the preamble to the Constitution of the World Health Organization, as adopted by the International Health Conference, New York, 19 June - 22 July 1946; signed on 22 July 1946 by the representatives of 61 States (Official Records of the World Health Organization, no. 2, p.100), and entered into force on 7 April 1948.

Graph on page 50 based on information from NHS Digital, licenced under the current version of the Open Government Licence.

Every effort has been made to locate copyright holders and obtain permission to reproduce sources.
For those sources where it has been difficult to trace the copyright holder of the work, we would be grateful
for information. If any copyright holder would like us to make an amendment to the acknowledgements,
please notify us and we will gladly update the book at the next reprint. Thank you.

ISBN: 978 1 78908 320 0
Printed by Elanders Ltd, Newcastle upon Tyne.
Clipart from Corel®

The Skeletal System

Welcome to the GCSE PE fun bus — first stop is the <u>skeleton</u>. It gives the body its <u>shape</u> and has loads of <u>jobs</u> to do. It's made up of various kinds of <u>bones</u>, all with their own function. Here we go...

The Skeleton has Different Functions

The skeleton does <u>more</u> than you might think to help your performance in sport. Its main functions are:

① <u>SUPPORT</u>:

1) The skeleton is a <u>rigid bone frame</u> for the rest of the body.
2) The skeleton <u>supports</u> the <u>soft tissues</u> like skin and muscle.

② <u>POSTURE</u>:

1) The skeleton gives our body the <u>correct shape</u>.
2) This helps you to have a good <u>posture</u>, which is <u>essential</u> in loads of sports.
3) E.g. good posture aids <u>performance</u> in <u>gymnastics</u>.

③ <u>PROTECTION</u>:

1) Bones are very <u>tough</u> — they <u>protect vital organs</u> like the <u>brain</u>, <u>heart</u> and <u>lungs</u>.
2) This allows you to <u>perform well</u> in sport without fear of serious <u>injury</u>.
3) E.g. the <u>skull</u> protects the brain, so you can <u>head</u> a football or take punches in a boxing match <u>without serious injury</u>.

④ <u>MOVEMENT</u>:

1) <u>Muscles</u>, <u>attached</u> to bones by <u>tendons</u>, can <u>move</u> bones at <u>joints</u>.
2) This movement is essential for good <u>performance</u> in sport.
3) There are different <u>types of movement</u> at the various <u>joints</u>, which are important in <u>different sports</u> (see p4).

⑤ <u>MAKING BLOOD CELLS</u>:

1) Some <u>bones</u> contain <u>bone marrow</u>, which makes the components of <u>blood</u>, including <u>red blood cells</u> (see p11).
2) <u>Red blood cells</u> are really <u>important</u> during exercise — they transport the <u>oxygen</u> that muscles need to move.
3) Athletes with <u>more</u> red blood cells <u>perform better</u> — <u>more oxygen</u> can be delivered to their muscles.

⑥ <u>MINERAL STORAGE</u>:

1) Bones store <u>minerals</u> like <u>calcium</u> and <u>phosphorus</u>.
2) These help with <u>bone strength</u> — so you're less likely to <u>break</u> a bone.
3) They're also needed for <u>muscle contraction</u> — so the body can <u>move</u>.

I bet you found that all extremely humerus...

It's really important that you remember all the different functions of the skeleton, and how each one helps your performance in physical activity and sport. Have a go at this Exam Practice Question to test your knowledge.

Q1   Using a practical example, explain how the skeleton's mineral storage function aids performance.   [2 marks]

The Skeletal System

Time for some more skeleton-related fun — this page'll give you a hand at remembering the names of some important bones in the body and what they do. I bet you can hardly wait...

Learn the Structure of the Skeleton

Luckily, you don't need to know all 206 bones in the human body — but you do need to know where some of the main ones are and examples of bones that allow movement or provide protection.

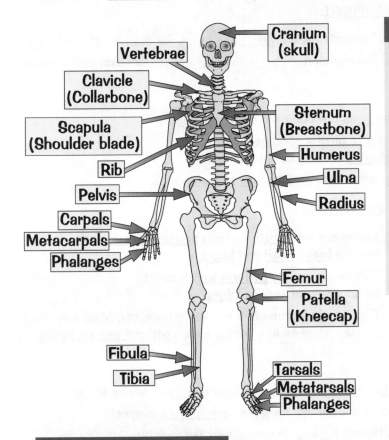

Cranium (skull)
Vertebrae
Clavicle (Collarbone)
Scapula (Shoulder blade)
Rib
Pelvis
Carpals
Metacarpals
Phalanges
Sternum (Breastbone)
Humerus
Ulna
Radius
Femur
Patella (Kneecap)
Fibula
Tibia
Tarsals
Metatarsals
Phalanges

Bones of the Head and Torso

Cranium — protects the brain.

Vertebrae — make up the vertebral column (spine). They protect the spinal cord.

Sternum and ribs — protect the heart and lungs. The ribs also protect the kidneys.

Scapula — protects the shoulder joint and has many muscles attached to it, helping arm and shoulder movement.

Clavicle — forms part of the shoulder joint to assist arm movement.

Pelvis — protects the reproductive organs and the bladder. It also has many muscles attached to it, helping leg movement.

Fluffy had a great time at the museum of natural history.

Bones of the Arms and Hands

Humerus — used by muscles to move the whole arm, e.g. swinging a badminton racket.

Ulna and radius — used by muscles to move the lower arm, e.g. bending at the elbow.

Carpals — form the wrist and give it stability, allowing movement of the hand.

Metacarpals — used by muscles to allow the hand to grip, e.g. to hold a cricket ball.

Phalanges — used by muscles to move and bend the fingers.

Bones of the Legs and Feet

Femur — used by muscles to move the whole leg, e.g. when running.

Fibula and tibia — used by muscles to move the lower leg, e.g. to kick a football.

Patella — protects the tendon that crosses the knee joint by stopping it rubbing against the femur.

Tarsals — bear the body's weight when on foot, e.g. during standing and running.

Metatarsals — used by muscles to move the foot, e.g. when jumping.

Phalanges — used by muscles to move and bend the toes.

Cranium, scapulas, patellas and toes, patellas and toes...

... Not quite as catchy. Now you know all about the skeleton's structure, give this Exam Practice Question a go.

Q1 Name the **two** bones of the lower leg. [2 marks]

Q2 Which **one** of these bones is found in the lower arm? **A** Femur **B** Humerus **C** Ulna **D** Tibia [1 mark]

The Skeletal System

Joints are really important parts of the skeleton — you need to know the different types, as well as what they are made of. Spoiler alert — they're made of more than just bones. Sorry to ruin the surprise of it all...

There are Different Kinds of Joint

1) Joints are any points where two or more bones meet. The bones that meet at a joint are called the articulating bones of the joint.
2) A synovial joint is a joint that allows a wide range of movement and has a joint capsule enclosing it.
3) Ball and socket and hinge joints are synovial joints.
4) A ball and socket joint allows movement in nearly every direction. The end of one bone fits into a cup-like area of another bone. E.g. at the hip joint, the head of the femur sits in the socket of the pelvis.
5) A hinge joint allows movement in only one direction. The joint is able to bend and straighten like the hinge on a door. E.g. the elbow joint between the humerus in the upper arm, and the radius and the ulna in the lower arm.
6) Here are a few examples of some of the major joints in the body, and their articulating bones.

Pelvis
Cartilage
Femur

Ball and Socket Joints	Hinge Joints
Hip — pelvis and femur	Knee — femur and tibia
Shoulder — humerus and scapula	Elbow — humerus, radius and ulna

Connective Tissues Join Muscle and Bones

There are three types of connective tissue you need to know about:

LIGAMENTS — hold bones together to restrict how much joints can move. This helps maintain the stability of the skeleton and prevents dislocation of joints. They're made of tough and fibrous tissue (like very strong string).

Ligaments also protect bones and joints by absorbing shock.

TENDONS — attach muscles to bones (or to other muscles) to allow bones to move when muscles contract.

CARTILAGE — acts as a cushion between bones to prevent damage during joint movement. It also aids the stability of a joint.

Learn the Structure of a Synovial Joint

1) The bones at a synovial joint are held together by ligaments.
2) The ends of the bones are covered with cartilage and are shaped so that they fit together and can move smoothly.
3) The synovial membrane releases synovial fluid into the joint capsule to lubricate (or 'oil') the joint, allowing it to move more easily.

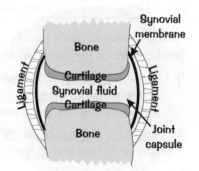
Bone
Synovial membrane
Ligament
Cartilage
Synovial fluid
Cartilage
Bone
Joint capsule

Two bones meet at a joint — they have an excellent time together...

Those connective tissues are really important — they all help your performance in physical activity and sport in a different way. Here are another couple of Exam Practice Questions on joints for you to have a go at.

Q1 State the joint type that allows the widest range of movement. [1 mark]

Q2 Explain the role of cartilage during physical activity. [2 marks]

The Skeletal System

Coming up on this page — a little more on joint movements, including examples of physical actions which involve each type of movement. Exciting stuff. Don't say I don't spoil you...

There are Different Kinds of Joint Movement

There are six joint movements that you need to know:

FLEXION

Closing a joint, e.g. the wrist movement during a basketball throw.

EXTENSION

Opening a joint, e.g. kicking a football.

ROTATION

Clockwise or anticlockwise movement, e.g. the leg movement during a turnout in ballet.

CIRCUMDUCTION

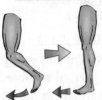

Movement of a limb, hand or foot in a circular motion, e.g. bowling a cricket ball overarm.

ABDUCTION

Moving away from an imaginary centre line, e.g. taking back a tennis racket before swinging it.

ADDUCTION

Moving towards an imaginary centre line, e.g. swinging a golf club.

Different Joint Types Allow Different Movements

You need to know which kinds of movement different types of joints allow.

joint type	examples	flexion and extension	adduction and abduction	rotation	circumduction
ball and socket	hip, shoulder	✓	✓	✓	✓
hinge	knee, elbow	✓	✗	✗	✗

During exercise, you'll usually use a combination of movement types, and often a combination of joints, either at the same time, or one after another. For example:

1) To do a push-up at the gym or a football throw-in, first you use flexion at the elbow to bend your arms. To straighten your arms again and complete the movements, you extend your arms at the elbow.

2) Running, kicking, basic squats and standing vertical jumps all use flexion and extension at the hip and knee.

3) Bowling in cricket involves the movement of the arm in a circular motion at the shoulder. This action is a combination of movements at the shoulder, including extension and rotation.

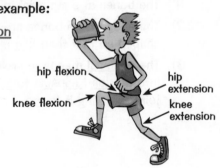

hip flexion
hip extension
knee flexion
knee extension

All this talk about joints is making me really hungry...

Make sure you learn all these joint and movement types for your exam. Now have a go at this Practice Question...

Q1   Analyse the movement that occurs at the elbow joint during a pass in netball.   [2 marks]

The Muscular System

The <u>skeletal system</u> can't make the body move <u>on its own</u> — it needs some help from the <u>muscular system</u>. Together, they're known as the <u>musculo-skeletal system</u>.

Muscles are Needed to Move Bones

1) The muscles that <u>enable movement</u> are attached to bones by <u>tendons</u> (see page 3).
2) When you <u>contract</u> a muscle (make it shorter) it pulls on the <u>tendon</u>, which pulls on the <u>bone</u>, making it <u>move</u>. Pretty nifty.
3) During <u>exercise</u>, muscles need <u>oxygen</u> so they can <u>move</u> the body.
4) When the heart beats, it <u>pumps blood</u> carrying oxygen to these muscles.

Each Muscle Group has a Specific Function

You need to learn the <u>names</u> of some <u>muscle groups</u>, and what their <u>main functions</u> are.

PECTORALS — <u>adduction</u> and <u>flexion</u> (horizontally) at the <u>shoulder</u>, e.g. during a forehand drive in tennis.

DELTOIDS — <u>flexion</u>, <u>extension</u>, <u>abduction</u> or <u>circumduction</u> at the <u>shoulder</u>, e.g. during front crawl in swimming.

TRAPEZIUS — <u>extension</u> at the <u>neck</u> (tilting the head back), e.g. preparing to head a football.

BICEPS — <u>flexion</u> at the <u>elbow</u>, e.g. when curling weights.

ABDOMINALS — <u>flexion</u> at the <u>waist</u>, e.g. during a sit-up.

TRICEPS — <u>extension</u> at the <u>elbow</u>, e.g. during a jump shot in netball.

QUADRICEPS — <u>extension</u> at the <u>knee</u>, e.g. when performing a drop kick in rugby.

LATISSIMUS DORSI — <u>extension</u>, <u>adduction</u> or <u>rotation</u> at the <u>shoulder</u>, e.g. during butterfly stroke in swimming.

Diagram labels: pectorals, deltoids, trapezius, biceps, abdominals, triceps, latissimus dorsi, quadriceps, gluteals, hamstrings, gastrocnemius (calf)

GLUTEALS — <u>extension</u>, <u>rotation</u>, and <u>abduction</u> of the leg at the <u>hip</u>, e.g. pushing the body forward when running.

GASTROCNEMIUS — pointing the <u>foot</u> downwards, e.g. when standing on the toes in ballet pointe work.

HAMSTRINGS — <u>flexion</u> at the <u>knee</u>, e.g. bringing the foot back before kicking a football.

Is that a bacon rope I see? Nope, it's a hamstring...

Take your time making sure you have learnt the different muscle groups properly — it could be easy to muddle up those biceps, triceps and quadriceps. When you're done, here are some Exam Practice Questions for you to try.

Q1 Name the **two** muscle groups found in the upper arm. [2 marks]

Q2 Where is the gastrocnemius muscle group found? [1 mark]

The Muscular System

Now on to more stuff about muscles — just what we were all hoping for. This page'll look at how muscles work together to produce different movement types at the joints in the body.

Antagonistic Muscles Work in Pairs

Muscles can only do one thing — pull. To make a joint move in two directions, you need two muscles that can pull in opposite directions.

1) Antagonistic muscles are pairs of muscles that work against each other.
2) One muscle contracts while the other one relaxes, and vice versa.
3) The muscle that's contracting is the agonist.
4) The muscle that's relaxing is the antagonist.
5) Each muscle is attached to two bones by tendons.
6) Only one of the bones connected at the joint actually moves.

Here, 'contracts' means 'shortens', and 'relaxes' means 'lengthens'. But you might see 'contracts' used to mean 'creates tension' — which muscles do when they shorten and lengthen.

During this antagonistic muscle action, other muscles can help the agonist to work properly by stabilising it where it attaches to the bone that doesn't move. These muscles are known as fixators.

- When the biceps are flexing the elbow joint, the deltoid and trapezius muscles act as fixators.
- For knee and hip movements, the abdominals act as fixators to stabilise the body.

You need to know some Antagonistic Muscle Pairs

There are antagonistic muscle pairs at different joints in the body:

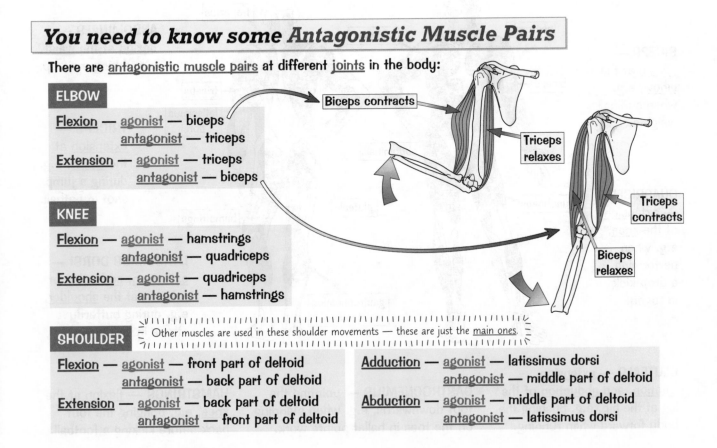

ELBOW

Flexion — agonist — biceps
      antagonist — triceps
Extension — agonist — triceps
      antagonist — biceps

KNEE

Flexion — agonist — hamstrings
      antagonist — quadriceps
Extension — agonist — quadriceps
      antagonist — hamstrings

Other muscles are used in these shoulder movements — these are just the main ones.

SHOULDER

Flexion — agonist — front part of deltoid
      antagonist — back part of deltoid
Extension — agonist — back part of deltoid
      antagonist — front part of deltoid

Adduction — agonist — latissimus dorsi
      antagonist — middle part of deltoid
Abduction — agonist — middle part of deltoid
      antagonist — latissimus dorsi

Dear Agonist Aunt, my PE revision is causing me grief...

This 'antagonistic muscle pair' stuff might seem a bit tricky, but just remember — the muscle that's the agonist in one movement will be the antagonist in the opposite movement. Here's an Exam Practice Question for you to try.

Q1 State the agonist muscle group that works to produce the knee
    movement when bringing the leg forward to kick a football.   [1 mark]

Lever Systems

When the <u>muscular</u> and <u>skeletal systems</u> work together, they create <u>lever systems</u> that help us to <u>move</u>.

Lever Systems Help the Body to Move

A <u>lever</u> is a <u>rigid bar</u> that moves about a <u>fixed point</u> when <u>force</u> is applied to it.
When a <u>muscle</u> pulls on a <u>bone</u> to move a body part about a <u>joint</u>, it uses the body part as a <u>lever</u>.
This lever makes up part of a <u>lever system</u> that has <u>four</u> different components:

1) The <u>lever arm</u> — the <u>bone</u> or <u>body part</u> being moved about a point.
   On a diagram of a lever system, it's shown as a <u>straight line</u>.
2) The <u>fulcrum</u> — the <u>joint</u> where the lever arm <u>pivots</u>. It's shown as a <u>triangle</u>.
3) The <u>effort</u> — the <u>force</u> applied by the <u>muscles</u> to the lever arm.
   It's shown by an <u>arrow</u> pointing in the direction of the force.
4) The <u>load</u> or <u>resistance</u> against the pull of the muscles on the lever arm. E.g. the weight of the body, or body part, or something being lifted. A <u>square</u> or an <u>arrow</u> is used to represent the load.

There are <u>three</u> types of lever system:

This is the <u>most common</u> type of lever in the body.

1ST CLASS — The <u>load</u> and <u>effort</u> are at <u>opposite ends</u> of the lever. The fulcrum is in the middle.

2ND CLASS — The <u>fulcrum</u> and <u>effort</u> are at <u>opposite ends</u> of the lever. The load is in the middle.

3RD CLASS — The <u>fulcrum</u> and <u>load</u> are at <u>opposite ends</u> of the lever. The effort is in the middle.

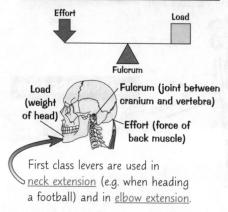

First class levers are used in <u>neck extension</u> (e.g. when heading a football) and in <u>elbow extension</u>.

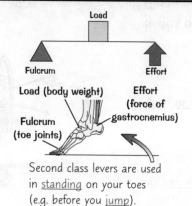

Second class levers are used in <u>standing</u> on your toes (e.g. before you <u>jump</u>).

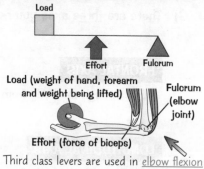

Third class levers are used in <u>elbow flexion</u> (e.g. lifting a weight) and in <u>flexion</u> and <u>extension</u> at the <u>shoulder</u>, <u>hip</u> and <u>knee</u>.

Levers can have Mechanical Advantage

1) If a lever provides <u>mechanical advantage</u>, it can move a <u>larger load</u> with a <u>smaller effort</u>.
2) For a lever providing mechanical advantage, the <u>effort</u> arm (the distance between the fulcrum and the effort) is <u>longer</u> than the <u>weight</u> (resistance) arm (the distance between the fulcrum and the load). Using the <u>formula</u> below for such a lever gives a <u>value</u> for mechanical advantage <u>greater than 1</u>.

<u>mechanical advantage</u> = effort arm ÷ weight (resistance) arm

3) <u>Second</u> class levers <u>always</u> provide mechanical advantage — the <u>effort arm</u> is always <u>longer</u> than the <u>weight arm</u>.
4) <u>First</u> class levers <u>can</u> provide mechanical advantage — it <u>depends</u> whether the fulcrum is <u>nearer</u> to the <u>effort</u> or to the <u>load</u>.
5) <u>Third</u> class levers <u>never</u> provide mechanical advantage.

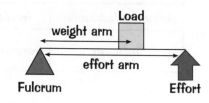

Moving joints — you'd better lever little space...

To remember the lever classes, use '1, 2, 3, F, L, E'. The letters tell you the middle component of each lever — for first class it's the <u>fulcrum</u>, for second class it's the <u>load</u>, and for third class it's the <u>effort</u>. Try this Practice Question.

Q1 Draw the lever system operating at the knee when standing up straight from a squat position. [1 mark]

Planes and Axes of Movement

It might seem a bit odd that there's a page about planes and axes in a PE book — but it'll all make sense soon. Basically, you can describe a body movement using the plane it moves in and the axis it moves around.

Movements Happen In Planes

1) A plane of movement is an imaginary flat surface which runs through the body.
2) Planes are used to describe the direction of a movement.
3) When you move a body part (or your whole body), it moves in a plane.
4) There are three planes of movement you need to know:

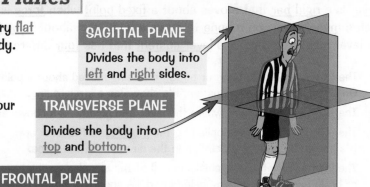

SAGITTAL PLANE
Divides the body into left and right sides.

TRANSVERSE PLANE
Divides the body into top and bottom.

FRONTAL PLANE
Divides the body's front and back.

Movements Happen Around Axes

1) An axis of rotation (two or more are called 'axes') is an imaginary line which runs through the body.
2) When a body part (or your whole body) moves, it moves around (or 'about') an axis.
3) There are three axes you need to know:

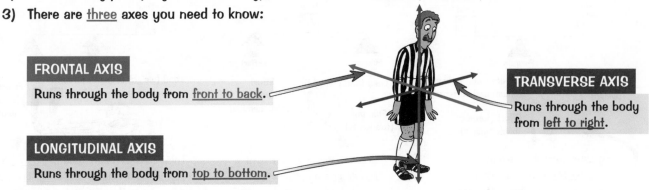

FRONTAL AXIS
Runs through the body from front to back.

TRANSVERSE AXIS
Runs through the body from left to right.

LONGITUDINAL AXIS
Runs through the body from top to bottom.

Movements use Different Planes and Axes

Every body movement uses both a plane and an axis.
Learn the plane and axis pairs for these movement types and sporting examples.

MOVEMENT TYPE	PLANE	AXIS	SPORT MOVEMENTS
flexion/extension	sagittal	transverse	tucked and piked somersaults, running, forward roll
abduction/adduction	frontal	frontal	cartwheel
rotation	transverse	longitudinal	full twist jump (trampolining), discus throw rotation, ice skating spin

Have a look at page 4 for more examples of the movement types.

These plane and axis pairs are always the same, e.g. movements that happen in the transverse plane always happen around the longitudinal axis.

Movement in planes — only when the seatbelt signs are off...

Don't forget, the plane of movement and axis of rotation combinations are always the same. So make sure you learn the pairs for your exam — it's easy marks. Have a go at this Exam Practice Question.

Q1 State the plane of movement and axis of rotation used during a star jump. [2 marks]

Revision Questions For Section One

That's <u>Anatomy and Physiology Part 1</u> wrapped up — time to see <u>how much you know</u> about the body.

- Try these questions and <u>tick off each one</u> when you <u>get it right</u>.
- When you've done <u>all the questions</u> for a topic and are <u>completely happy</u> with it, tick off the topic.
- The answers can all be found by <u>looking back over pages 1 to 8</u>.

The Skeletal System (p1-4) ☑

1) Name the six main functions of the skeleton.
2) What is the clavicle commonly known as?
3) Give two places where the phalanges are found.
4) Which two bones meet to make the shoulder joint?
5) What is the function of:
   a) Cartilage?
   b) Ligaments?
   c) Tendons?
6) What is the definition of a synovial joint?
7) What is abduction?

The Muscular System (p5-6) ☑

8) How does a muscle contracting cause a bone to move?
9) Give two examples of muscle groups found in the leg.
10) What is a fixator muscle?
11) Which two muscles make up the antagonistic muscle pair operating at the elbow joint?

Lever Systems (p7) ☑

12) Name the four components of a lever system.
13) Give an example of a movement that uses a third class lever.
14) State the class of each of the levers below.

a)   b)   c)

15) Give two examples of first class levers in the body.
16) Which lever class is used during elbow flexion?
17) Explain what is meant if a lever system in the body has a mechanical advantage.
18) Third class levers always provide mechanical advantage — true or false?

Planes and Axes of Movement (p8) ☑

19) What is a plane of movement?
20) Which plane of movement divides the left and right sides of the body?
21) What is an axis of rotation?
22) Which axis of rotation runs through the body from top to bottom?
23) Which plane of movement and axis of rotation are used during a cartwheel?

The Cardiovascular System

Your cardiovascular system's job is to <u>move blood</u> around your body. As the blood travels around, it does loads of really <u>useful stuff</u> to help you <u>take part</u> in physical activity and sport. Read on to find out more...

The Cardiovascular System has Two Main Functions

TRANSPORT OF SUBSTANCES
<u>Transporting</u> things around the body in the bloodstream, like <u>oxygen</u>, <u>carbon dioxide</u>, and <u>nutrients</u> (e.g. glucose). This gives the <u>muscles</u> what they need to <u>release energy</u> to <u>move</u> during exercise (and takes away any <u>waste</u> products).

Have a look at p13 for more about how muscles use oxygen and glucose.

TEMPERATURE CONTROL
Moving more blood nearer the skin <u>cools</u> the body more quickly. This means you can exercise for a <u>long time</u> without <u>overheating</u>.

Learn How the Heart Pumps Blood Around the Body

1) The <u>cardiovascular system</u> is made up of three main parts — the <u>heart</u>, <u>blood</u> and <u>blood vessels</u>.
2) During any kind of <u>physical activity</u>, blood needs to <u>circulate</u> around the body to deliver <u>oxygen</u> and <u>glucose</u> to your <u>muscles</u>, and to <u>take carbon dioxide away</u> from them.
3) The cardiovascular system is a <u>double-circulatory system</u> — this means <u>there are two circuits</u>. The <u>pulmonary circuit</u> connects the <u>lungs</u> to the heart and the <u>systemic circuit</u> connects the <u>rest of the body</u> to the heart.

Lungs

Rest of Body

PULMONARY CIRCUIT

* <u>Deoxygenated blood</u> enters the <u>right ventricle</u> through the <u>tricuspid valve</u>.
* The right ventricle <u>contracts</u>, pushing the blood through the <u>right semi-lunar valve</u> into the <u>pulmonary artery</u>, which carries the blood to the <u>lungs</u> to be <u>oxygenated</u>.
* <u>Oxygenated blood</u> from the <u>lungs</u> enters the <u>left atrium</u> through the <u>pulmonary veins</u>.

Pressure in the heart causes the valves to open. They close to stop blood flowing the wrong way.

SYSTEMIC CIRCUIT

* <u>Oxygenated blood</u> enters the <u>left ventricle</u> through the <u>bicuspid valve</u>.
* The left ventricle <u>contracts</u>, pushing the blood through the <u>left semi-lunar valve</u> into the <u>aorta</u> (an <u>artery</u>), which carries the <u>oxygenated blood</u> to the rest of the <u>body</u> — including the muscles.
* When the muscles have <u>used</u> the oxygen in the blood, it becomes <u>deoxygenated</u>. It then enters the <u>right atrium</u> through the <u>vena cava</u> vein.

The word for more than one atrium is 'atria'.

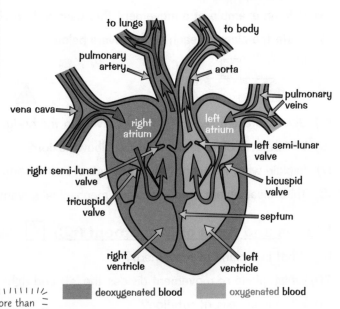

to lungs · to body · pulmonary artery · aorta · vena cava · right atrium · left atrium · pulmonary veins · left semi-lunar valve · right semi-lunar valve · bicuspid valve · tricuspid valve · septum · right ventricle · left ventricle

deoxygenated blood   oxygenated blood

The heart — it's all just pump and circumstance...

The 'left's and 'right's on the heart diagram mean on the person whose heart it is — that's why they're reversed. Now, get learning what all the bits of the cardiovascular system do, and try this Practice Question.

Q1   Analyse the role of the pulmonary artery in physical activity and sport.   [2 marks]

The Cardiovascular System

Your cardiovascular system has different types of blood vessels that carry blood around your body.
This page'll tell you all about them, as well as some measures of blood flow that you need to know.

Arteries, Veins and Capillaries Carry Blood

1) Blood vessels transport blood — they have a hollow centre called the lumen so blood can flow through.

2) Different types of blood vessel are suited to different roles:

ARTERIES — carry blood away from the heart. All arteries carry oxygenated blood except for the pulmonary artery. Their thick, muscular walls allow them to carry blood flowing at high pressure.

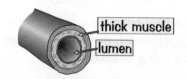
thick muscle
lumen

The muscle in the walls of arteries and veins allows them to widen and narrow to control blood flow (see p15).

Blood pressure is how strongly the blood presses against the walls of blood vessels.

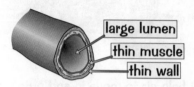
large lumen
thin muscle
thin wall

VEINS — carry blood towards the heart. They have valves to stop blood flowing the wrong way. All veins carry deoxygenated blood, except for the pulmonary veins. They carry blood at low pressure, so they have thinner walls and less muscle than arteries.

CAPILLARIES — carry blood through the body to exchange gases and nutrients with the body's tissues. They have very thin walls so substances can easily pass through. They're also very narrow, which means lots of them can fit into the body's tissues — giving them a large surface area to let gas exchange happen more easily. It also means that blood can only flow through them slowly — giving more time for gas exchange.

thin wall

The Volume of Blood Flowing can Change

1) Your heart rate is the number of times your heart beats per minute. An adult's resting heart rate (their heart rate when they aren't exercising) is usually about 60-80 bpm (beats per minute).

2) Your stroke volume is the amount of blood each ventricle pumps with each contraction (or heartbeat).

3) Your cardiac output is the volume of blood pumped by a ventricle per minute. Here's the formula to calculate cardiac output:

> cardiac output (Q) = heart rate × stroke volume

Red Blood Cells Carry Oxygen

Lots of different things make up the blood in your body. The red blood cells are the most important component when it comes to taking part in physical activity.

RED BLOOD CELLS — carry oxygen and transport it around the body to be used to release energy needed by muscles during physical activity. They also carry carbon dioxide to the lungs. Haemoglobin (a protein in red blood cells) stores oxygen and carbon dioxide.

What do vampires cross the sea in? Blood vessels...

If you're struggling to remember whether veins and arteries carry blood to or from the heart, just remember — arteries carry blood away from the heart. Here's a Practice Question for you to have a go at.

Q1 Explain the role of capillaries during physical activity. [2 marks]

The Respiratory System

You'll probably recognise most of this stuff from biology — but there's no harm in a quick recap.

Learn the Structure of the Respiratory System

The respiratory system is everything you use to breathe.
It's found in the chest cavity — the area inside the chest.

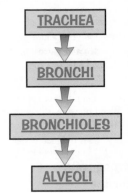

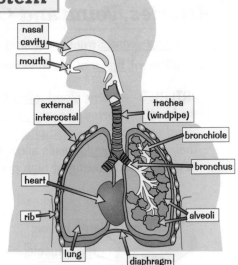

TRACHEA → BRONCHI → BRONCHIOLES → ALVEOLI

1) Air passes through the nose or mouth and then on to the trachea.

2) The trachea splits into two tubes called bronchi (each one is a 'bronchus') — one going to each lung.

3) The bronchi split into progressively smaller tubes called bronchioles.

4) The bronchioles finally end at small bags called alveoli (each one is an 'alveolus') where gases are exchanged (see below).

The diaphragm and external intercostal muscles (the respiratory muscles) help air to move in and out:

- When you breathe in, the diaphragm and external intercostals contract to move the ribcage upwards and expand the chest cavity. This draws air into your lungs.
- When you breathe out, the diaphragm and the external intercostals relax, moving the ribcage down and shrinking the chest cavity. This forces air back out of the lungs the same way it came in.

Oxygen and Carbon Dioxide are Exchanged in the Alveoli

1) The cardiovascular and respiratory systems have to work together to get oxygen to the muscles, and carbon dioxide away from them. They do this by exchanging gases between the alveoli and capillaries surrounding them.

The cardiovascular and respiratory systems together make up the cardio-respiratory system.

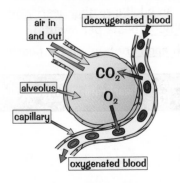

1) Oxygenated blood delivers oxygen and collects carbon dioxide as it circulates around the body. Deoxygenated blood returns to the heart and is then pumped to the lungs.

2) In the lungs, carbon dioxide moves from the blood in the capillaries into the alveoli so it can be breathed out.

3) Oxygen from the air you breathe into the lungs moves across from the alveoli to the red blood cells in the capillaries.

4) The oxygenated blood returns to the heart and is pumped to the rest of the body. The red blood cells carry the oxygen around the body and deliver it where it's needed, e.g. the muscles.

2) Alveoli are surrounded by lots of capillaries, giving them a large blood supply to exchange gases with.

3) They also have a large surface area and moist, thin walls — so gases can easily pass through them.

4) This exchange of gases happens through a process called diffusion. This means the gases move down a concentration gradient — from a place of higher concentration to a place of lower concentration:

IN ALVEOLUS
High concentration of O_2
Low concentration of CO_2

DIFFUSION OF O_2 →
← DIFFUSION OF CO_2

IN CAPILLARY
Low concentration of O_2
High concentration of CO_2

O_2 = oxygen
CO_2 = carbon dioxide

Air we go — keeping trachea respiratory system...

So, diffusion is pretty impressive, eh? I bet you'll be impressed with this Exam Practice Question, too.

Q1 Describe how deoxygenated blood becomes oxygenated. [3 marks]

The Respiratory System

You might have noticed that you take <u>bigger breaths</u> when you <u>exercise</u>. That's just 'cos the air we <u>breathe in</u> contains the <u>stuff</u> we need <u>more</u> of for <u>exercise</u>, and the air we <u>breathe out</u> contains the <u>stuff we don't want</u>.

Aerobic Exercise — With Oxygen

1) <u>All</u> the living cells in your body need <u>energy</u>. Normally the body uses <u>oxygen</u> to release <u>energy</u> from <u>glucose</u> (a <u>sugar</u> found in food). This is called <u>aerobic respiration</u>.

> Glucose + Oxygen   ➡   Carbon dioxide + Water + Energy

Carbon dioxide and water are <u>by-products</u> of aerobic respiration.

2) If your body's keeping up with the <u>oxygen demand</u> of its cells, it means there's enough oxygen available for aerobic respiration.

3) Exercise where your body can <u>keep up</u> with oxygen demand is called <u>aerobic</u>.

> <u>AEROBIC EXERCISE</u>: 'with oxygen'. When exercise is <u>not too fast</u> and is <u>steady</u>, the heart can supply all the oxygen that the working muscles need.

4) You <u>breathe out</u> the carbon dioxide through your lungs, while the water is lost as <u>sweat</u>, <u>urine</u>, or in the <u>air</u> you breathe out.

5) As long as your muscles are <u>supplied with enough oxygen</u>, you can do aerobic exercise — so if you're exercising for <u>long periods</u>, you'll be producing your energy <u>aerobically</u>.

6) Aerobic respiration is how <u>marathon runners</u> get their energy — it's the <u>most efficient</u> way to get it.

Anaerobic Exercise — Without Oxygen

1) During <u>vigorous exercise</u>, your body <u>can't</u> supply all the oxygen needed. When this happens, your muscles release energy <u>without</u> using oxygen in a different process called <u>anaerobic respiration</u>.

> Glucose   ➡   Energy + Lactic acid

Lactic acid is a by-product of anaerobic respiration — you need oxygen to remove it (see next page).

2) Exercise where your body has to do this is called <u>anaerobic</u>.

> <u>ANAEROBIC EXERCISE</u>: 'without oxygen'. When exercise duration is <u>short</u> and at <u>high intensity</u>, the heart and lungs can't supply blood and oxygen to muscles as fast as the cells need them.

3) The <u>lack of oxygen</u> during anaerobic respiration means it can only provide <u>energy</u> for <u>short periods</u> of time — so you can't exercise at <u>high intensity</u> for very long.

4) <u>Sprinters</u> get their energy anaerobically — they have to run <u>quickly</u> for <u>short durations</u>.

You Can Measure Your Breathing in Different Ways

1) Your <u>breathing rate</u> is the number of breaths you take per minute.

2) You can also measure the <u>amount of air</u> you breathe in or out during <u>one breath</u> — this is known as your <u>tidal volume</u>.

3) The <u>volume</u> of air you breathe in or out each <u>minute</u> is called your <u>minute ventilation</u>.

Have you met Anna Robic? She's an excellent sprinter...

You can adapt your training to make your body better at exercising either aerobically or anaerobically — for example, circuit training stations could be chosen to focus on anaerobic fitness (see page 28).

Q1   Justify why a 100-metre sprint would be anaerobic exercise.

                                                                [3 marks]

Short-Term Effects of Exercise

During exercise, your <u>heart</u> and <u>lungs</u> work <u>extra hard</u> to try and get <u>more oxygen</u> to your <u>muscles</u> so they can work properly. But if your muscles work <u>too hard</u>, they can get a bit <u>tired</u> — poor things.

There are Short-Term Effects on the Muscular System

1) When you exercise, your muscles release <u>extra energy</u> for movement. Producing this energy also <u>generates heat</u>, which increases <u>muscle temperature</u>.

2) Also, during <u>anaerobic</u> activity, your muscles produce <u>lactic acid</u>.

3) If you use your muscles <u>anaerobically</u> for too long, lactic acid starts to <u>build up</u>. This leads to a rise in the <u>lactate levels</u> in the body — <u>lactate accumulation</u>.

4) Lactic acid build-up makes your muscles <u>painful</u> and causes <u>muscle fatigue</u> (tiredness).

5) If your muscles are <u>fatigued</u>, they need <u>oxygen</u> to <u>remove the lactic acid</u> and <u>recover</u>. The amount of <u>oxygen</u> you need is the <u>oxygen debt</u>.

6) To <u>repay oxygen debt</u>, you'll need to <u>slow down</u> or <u>stop</u> the activity you're doing for a while, which can have a <u>negative</u> impact on your <u>performance</u>.

7) During a training session where you do <u>anaerobic activity</u>, you'll need to have periods of <u>rest</u> or <u>low intensity</u> exercise before you can work anaerobically again.

There are Short-Term Effects on the Respiratory System

1) During exercise, <u>muscles</u> such as the <u>pectorals</u> and the <u>sternocleidomastoid</u> (in the neck) <u>expand</u> your lungs more to let in <u>extra air</u>. Muscles in your <u>abdomen</u> also work to pull your <u>ribcage</u> down and shrink the chest cavity quicker, so you <u>breathe out</u> faster.

2) These changes help to increase your <u>tidal volume</u> and <u>respiratory rate</u> ← (the <u>number of breaths</u> per minute), which leads to an increase in your <u>minute ventilation</u> (or 'minute volume').

> Respiratory rate and breathing rate are the same thing.

3) This means <u>more oxygen</u> is taken in and transferred to the blood, which helps to meet the <u>increased demand</u> for oxygen in the <u>muscles</u> during physical activity.

4) It also helps you to <u>breathe out</u> the extra <u>carbon dioxide</u> produced during aerobic respiration.

5) These changes allow you to do <u>aerobic activity</u> for <u>long periods</u> of time.

6) If you've been doing <u>anaerobic activity</u>, your breathing rate and depth will remain higher than normal until you've taken in enough <u>oxygen</u> to 'pay off' your <u>oxygen debt</u>.

The Effects aren't Always the Same

1) Activities have different levels of <u>intensity</u>, so when you are describing the effects on the <u>respiratory system</u> during an activity think about how the intensity <u>changes</u>.

2) The changes to the respiratory system will be more <u>extreme</u> if you exercise really <u>intensely</u> — you'll breathe <u>deeper</u> and <u>quicker</u>.

3) <u>Light exercise</u> isn't going to have as much of an <u>effect</u>.

4) For example, an elite rower will have a sharp <u>increase</u> in respiratory rate and minute ventilation <u>during a race</u>. There will not be as big a change to the respiratory system of someone having a nice, <u>leisurely</u> row on a lake.

5) It's the same for other <u>activities</u> — the changes in the respiratory system of a gymnast performing <u>static stretching</u> are not going to be as significant as those in a dancer performing an <u>energetic routine</u>.

Breathe iiiiiiiiiiiiiiiin — and oooooooouuuuuuut...

Make sure you understand all these short-term changes that happen when you exercise. You're very likely to have to come up with some of them in the exam Here's an Exam Practice Question to have a go at.

Q1 Explain the change to tidal volume during exercise. [2 marks]

Short-Term Effects of Exercise

Your cardiovascular system works extra hard during exercise to make sure your muscles get what they need to work properly. This includes using your blood vessels to send your blood where it's needed the most.

There are Short-Term Effects on the Cardiovascular System

1) During exercise, your heart rate and stroke volume both increase.

2) This leads to an increase in your cardiac output.

3) An increase in cardiac output increases the blood and oxygen supply to your muscles — so they can release the energy they need for physical activity.

4) It also removes more carbon dioxide from the muscles and takes it to the lungs to be breathed out.

5) Your heart rate, stroke volume and cardiac output will remain higher than normal after exercise until any oxygen debt is paid off.

If you've forgotten the definitions of any of these terms, have a look at page 11 again.

> The harder you're exercising, the higher your heart rate, stroke volume and cardiac output will be. So if you're only doing very light exercise, they'll be lower than if you were doing really strenuous exercise.

Your Blood Vessels Change when you Exercise

When you exercise, blood is redistributed around the body to increase the supply of oxygen to your muscles — this is known as 'vascular shunting'.

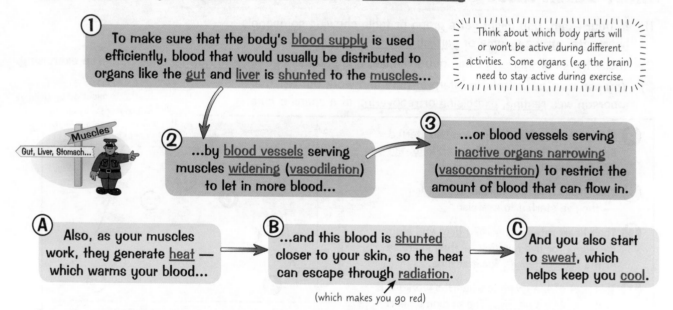

① To make sure that the body's blood supply is used efficiently, blood that would usually be distributed to organs like the gut and liver is shunted to the muscles...

Think about which body parts will or won't be active during different activities. Some organs (e.g. the brain) need to stay active during exercise.

② ...by blood vessels serving muscles widening (vasodilation) to let in more blood...

③ ...or blood vessels serving inactive organs narrowing (vasoconstriction) to restrict the amount of blood that can flow in.

Ⓐ Also, as your muscles work, they generate heat — which warms your blood...

Ⓑ ...and this blood is shunted closer to your skin, so the heat can escape through radiation.
(which makes you go red)

Ⓒ And you also start to sweat, which helps keep you cool.

The amount of blood that's redistributed depends on how intensely you're exercising. During light exercise, only a small amount of blood is shunted towards your working muscles — if you're exercising really hard, a lot more blood is shunted.

Romantic comedies — exercise for your heart...

Remember, vascular shunting happens during exercise because your muscles need blood more than some of your organs do. And this couldn't happen without vasodilation and vasoconstriction. To the Practice Questions...

Q1 Copy and complete the following statements about the short-term effects of exercise.

During exercise, the .... and stroke volume increase. This leads to an increase in the .... output so more oxygenated .... is delivered to the muscles. [3 marks]

Q2 Explain why blood vessels to the stomach narrow during physical activity and sport. [2 marks]

Short-Term Effects of Exercise

This page'll show you how the <u>cardiovascular</u> and <u>respiratory</u> systems <u>team up</u> to help you exercise.
It'll also give you some handy tips on how to <u>interpret exercise data</u> that you might see in the exam.

The Cardiovascular and Respiratory Systems Work Together

1) During exercise (and immediately after), <u>more oxygen</u> is delivered to the muscles than normal. Extra <u>carbon dioxide</u> is also taken away from them and <u>breathed out</u>.

2) The <u>cardiovascular</u> and <u>respiratory</u> systems work together to make this happen. When you exercise:

MORE O_2 DELIVERED

1) <u>Breathing rate</u> and <u>depth</u> increase, so more oxygen is delivered to the <u>alveoli</u> in the lungs.

2) <u>Cardiac output</u> also increases — so <u>blood</u> passes through the lungs at a <u>faster rate</u>, and picks up the <u>extra oxygen</u> from the <u>alveoli</u>. It's then delivered to the <u>muscles</u>.

MORE CO_2 REMOVED

1) Increased <u>cardiac output</u> means that the blood can transport <u>carbon dioxide</u> from the <u>muscles</u> to the <u>lungs</u> more <u>quickly</u>.

2) Here it moves into the <u>alveoli</u>, and the higher <u>breathing rate</u> and <u>depth</u> allow it to be quickly <u>breathed out</u>.

3) These changes create a <u>high concentration gradient</u> — after you breathe in, there's a lot <u>more oxygen</u> in the <u>alveoli</u> than the capillaries, and a lot <u>more carbon dioxide</u> in the <u>capillaries</u> than the alveoli.

4) This causes <u>diffusion</u> of the gases to happen <u>much more quickly</u> during exercise.

For more on diffusion, have a look at page 12.

5) These processes help you to release enough <u>energy</u> to <u>exercise</u> aerobically and to <u>recover</u> from <u>oxygen debt</u> after anaerobic activity (see p14).

Short-Term Effects can be shown Graphically

1) In your exam, you might get a graph or table showing someone's <u>heart rate</u>, <u>stroke volume</u> or <u>cardiac output</u> during a workout.

2) These things all <u>increase</u> when you exercise, and gradually go <u>back to normal</u> once you stop exercising.

3) You can use these facts to <u>interpret</u> data and work out whether a person was <u>resting</u>, <u>exercising</u> or <u>recovering</u> at a specific time.

Your <u>heart rate</u> might go up slightly just <u>before</u> you start exercising — this is known as an <u>anticipatory rise</u>.

Ⓐ This point is <u>before</u> the person has started exercising. Their heart rate is at its <u>lowest point</u> — it's their <u>resting heart rate</u>.

Ⓑ Their heart rate has started to <u>increase</u> — they've started to exercise.

Ⓒ Their heart rate reaches <u>130 bpm</u> and <u>stays the same</u> for five minutes — they exercise at the <u>same intensity</u> for that time.

Ⓓ This part of the graph is when the workout is at its <u>highest intensity</u>. The person's heart rate is at its <u>highest</u> point on the graph.

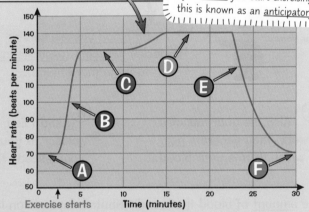

Ⓔ Their heart rate is <u>decreasing</u> — exercise has <u>stopped</u>, or they're completing a <u>cool down</u>. Their heart rate <u>stays fairly high</u> for a while to help with <u>recovery</u>.

Ⓕ They've returned to their <u>resting</u> heart rate of 70 beats per minute.

Graphs and tables? I didn't sign up for extra maths lessons...

I bet you weren't pleased to see a graph on this page, but it's not too bad. If you get given any heart rate, stroke volume or cardiac output data in your exam, remember that they all go up during exercise, and back down after. Then you can work out what was going on when the values were recorded. Try this Practice Question.

Q1 The table on the right shows an athlete's stroke volume recorded three times during a training session. Identify which value was recorded:

| 94 cm³ | 141 cm³ | 63 cm³ |

a) before exercise started [1 mark]   b) during high-intensity exercise [1 mark]

Long-Term Effects of Exercise

<u>Exercising regularly</u> eventually leads to loads of <u>adaptations</u> in the body's systems. These benefit your <u>health</u> and different components of <u>fitness</u> (see pages 19-21), which will help improve your <u>performance</u>.

Exercise Improves the Musculo-Skeletal System

1) Doing regular exercise will make your muscles <u>thicker</u> and your <u>muscle girth</u> larger — which can change your <u>body shape</u>.

2) This thickening of muscles is called <u>hypertrophy</u>. It happens to all muscles when they're exercised, including your <u>heart</u>.

3) The thicker a muscle is, the <u>more strongly</u> it can <u>contract</u> — so this increases your muscular <u>strength</u>.

4) Hypertrophy also improves your <u>muscular endurance</u>, and increases your <u>resistance to fatigue</u> — so you can use your muscles for <u>longer</u>.

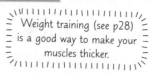

Weight training (see p28) is a good way to make your muscles thicker.

MUSCLE HYPERTROPHY

Boring trophy   Hypertrophy

INCREASED BONE DENSITY

1) The <u>denser</u> your bones, the <u>stronger</u> they are.

2) <u>Exercise</u> usually puts <u>stress</u> or forces through bones, and will cause the body to <u>strengthen</u> those bones.

3) Stronger bones are <u>less likely</u> to <u>break</u> or <u>fracture</u>.

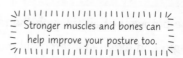

Stronger muscles and bones can help improve your posture too.

Exercise Improves the Cardio-Respiratory System

BIGGER/STRONGER HEART

1) Your heart is just a <u>muscle</u> — when you exercise, it <u>adapts</u> and gets <u>bigger</u> and <u>stronger</u>.

2) A bigger, stronger heart will contract more <u>strongly</u> and pump <u>more</u> blood with each beat — so your <u>resting stroke volume</u> and <u>maximum cardiac output</u> will <u>increase</u>.

3) A larger <u>stroke volume</u> means your heart has to beat <u>less often</u> to pump the same amount of blood around your body — your <u>resting heart rate decreases</u>.

LARGER LUNG CAPACITY

1) Your <u>respiratory muscles</u> (the <u>diaphragm</u> and <u>intercostal</u> muscles) get <u>stronger</u> — so they can make your <u>chest cavity larger</u>. The number of <u>alveoli</u> in your lungs also <u>increases</u>.

2) This increases your maximum <u>tidal volume</u> and <u>minute ventilation</u> during exercise — you can breathe in <u>more air</u>.

3) This means you can get <u>more oxygen</u> into your lungs and bloodstream per breath — so you can take in the same amount of oxygen with a <u>lower breathing rate</u>.

MORE CAPILLARIES

There is an <u>increase</u> in the number of <u>capillaries</u> in the <u>muscles</u> and at the <u>alveoli</u>. This increases the <u>blood supply</u> to the muscles, so they receive <u>more oxygen</u>. This is called <u>capillarisation</u>.

These changes increase your <u>aerobic capacity</u> — the body's ability to get <u>oxygen</u> to the <u>muscles</u>. This means you can exercise more <u>intensely</u> and for <u>longer</u>, as well as <u>recover more quickly</u> after exercise.

Breaking news — exercise is good for you...

To get all these lovely long-term effects, you'll need to rest after exercise so that you can recover and let your body adapt to any changes. Here's the last Exam Practice Question in this section for you to try. Have fun...

Q1   Describe what muscle hypertrophy is and how it would benefit a weightlifter.   [2 marks]

Revision Questions For Section Two

Well, that's <u>Anatomy and Physiology</u> all wrapped up — time to see <u>how much you know</u> about the body.
- Try these questions and <u>tick off each one</u> when you <u>get it right</u>.
- When you've done <u>all the questions</u> for a topic and are <u>completely happy</u> with it, tick off the topic.
- The answers can all be found by <u>looking back over pages 10 to 17</u>.

The Cardiovascular System (p10-11)

1) What are two main functions of the cardiovascular system?
2) Which vein does deoxygenated blood pass through to enter the heart?
3) The pulmonary artery carries oxygenated blood to the rest of the body. TRUE or FALSE?
4) Name the three main types of blood vessel found in the body.
5) Which type of blood vessel has a thick muscular wall?
6) What is cardiac output and how is it calculated?
7) Which type of cell carries oxygen around the body?

The Respiratory System (12-13)

8) Describe the pathway of air through the respiratory system.
9) The diaphragm and external intercostal muscles contract to expand the chest cavity. TRUE or FALSE?
10) Explain how oxygen and carbon dioxide are exchanged between the alveoli and capillaries.
11) Describe aerobic and anaerobic exercise.
12) What is the main fuel source used in both aerobic and anaerobic activity?
13) Is really vigorous exercise likely to be aerobic or anaerobic?
14) What is the by-product of anaerobic respiration?
15) Describe what is meant by tidal volume.

The Short-Term Effects of Exercise (p14-16)

16) Why do muscles become fatigued during anaerobic activity, and how do they recover?
17) Explain why your tidal volume and respiratory rate increase during exercise.
18) Why does tidal volume and breathing rate often remain higher for a short time after exercise?
19) Explain how the narrowing and widening of blood vessels affects blood flow.
20) Describe what is meant by vascular shunting.
21) What would happen to a graph of someone's cardiac output if they started exercising?

The Long-Term Effects of Exercise (p17)

22) What is muscle hypertrophy and why does it happen?
23) How does regular exercise benefit the bones?
24) Explain why regular exercise leads to increased oxygen supply to the muscles during exercise.
25) What is the benefit of having a bigger stroke volume?
26) What is capillarisation?

Components of Fitness

We'll start with telekinesis, then a bit of mind-reading... Sorry, I thought this section was Psychical Training. Fitness can be split up into different components. Here are the first three, so hop to it and get learning...

Cardiovascular Endurance — *Getting Energy using Oxygen*

1) Your heart and lungs work together to keep your muscles supplied with oxygen. Your muscles can then get energy from aerobic respiration (see p13). The harder you work your muscles, the more oxygen they need.

> CARDIOVASCULAR ENDURANCE or STAMINA is the ability to continue exercising while getting energy for muscular movement from aerobic respiration.

2) So if you have a high level of cardiovascular endurance, your body is able to supply the oxygen that your muscles need to do moderately intense, aerobic, whole-body exercise for a long time.

3) Most sports require good cardiovascular endurance. For example, a squash player needs to be able to keep up a fast pace all game. If a tennis player finds they are getting tired and losing points late on in a match, they will want to work on their cardiovascular endurance.

4) A high level of cardiovascular endurance is particularly important for endurance sports like long-distance running, or cycling.

Muscular Endurance — *How Long 'til You get Tired*

1) When you work your muscles they can get tired and start to feel heavy and weak (fatigued).

> MUSCULAR ENDURANCE is the ability to repeatedly use muscles over a long time, without getting tired.

2) Muscular endurance is really important in any physical activity where you're using the same muscles over and over again — e.g. in racquet sports like tennis or squash where you have to repeatedly swing your arm.

3) It's also dead important towards the end of any long-distance race — rowers and cyclists need muscular endurance for a strong sprint finish.

Dave's muscular endurance was low — his arm felt heavy after 3 swigs of tea.

Strength — *the Force a Muscle can Exert*

1) Strength is just how strong your muscles are.

> STRENGTH is the maximum amount of force that a muscle or muscle group can apply against a resistance.

You might see 'muscular strength' instead of 'strength' — don't panic though, it's the same thing.

2) It's very important in sports where you need to lift, push or pull things using a lot of force, like weightlifting and judo.

3) Sports that require you to hold your own body weight also need a lot of strength — like the parallel bars and rings in gymnastics.

4) There are different types of strength. Two examples are:

- Maximal strength is the most amount of force a muscle group can create in a single movement.

- Explosive strength uses a muscle's strength in a short, fast burst — it's similar to power (see p20).

'Be strong Luke — apply the force against a resistance...'

Make sure you're specific about how components of fitness are used in different activities — e.g. instead of just saying 'strength helps in gymnastics' say 'strength helps the gymnast hold their body weight on the parallel bars'.

Q1 Analyse the importance of muscular endurance for a long-distance cyclist.   [3 marks]

Components of Fitness

Three more components of fitness on this page: speed, power and flexibility. Learn what they are — then make sure you learn what sports and activities each one's important in as well. Right, here we go...

Speed — How Quickly

1) Speed is a measure of how quickly you can do something.

2) This might be a measure of how quickly you cover a distance. It could also be how quickly you can carry out a movement, e.g. how quickly you can throw a punch.

3) To work out speed, you just divide the distance covered by the time taken to do it.

4) Speed is important in lots of activities, from the obvious like a 100 m sprint, to the less obvious (like the speed a hockey player can swing their arm to whack a ball across the pitch).

> SPEED is the rate at which someone is able to move, or to cover a distance in a given amount of time.

Power Means Speed and Strength Together

> POWER is being able to exert as much strength as possible in the shortest time possible

> power = strength × speed

Most sports need power for some things. It's important for throwing, hitting, sprinting and jumping — e.g. in the long jump, both the sprint run-up and the take-off from the board require power.

Here are some more examples:

I have the power.

SPORT	YOU NEED POWER TO...
Football	...shoot
Golf	...drive
Table tennis	...smash
Tennis	...serve and smash
Cricket	...bowl fast and bat

Coordination and balance (see next page) also help make the most of power — an uncoordinated or off-balance action will not be as powerful.

Flexibility — Range of Movement

1) Flexibility is to do with how far your joints move. This depends on the type of joint and the 'stretchiness' of the muscles around it.

> FLEXIBILITY is the amount of movement possible at a joint.

2) It's often forgotten about, but flexibility is dead useful for any physical activity. Here's why...

He'll bend over backwards to help you, you know.

So I've heard.

- **FEWER INJURIES:**
  If you're flexible, you're less likely to pull or strain a muscle or stretch too far and injure yourself.

- **BETTER PERFORMANCE:**
  You can't do some sporting actions without being flexible — e.g. the splits in gymnastics.
  Flexibility makes you more efficient in other sports so you use less energy — e.g. swimmers with better flexibility can move their arms further around their shoulders. This makes their strokes longer and smoother.

- **BETTER POSTURE:**
  Bad posture can impair breathing and damage your spine.
  More flexibility means a better posture and fewer aches and pains.

It took me years to get this flexible.

Revise more I tell you — sorry, all this power's gone to my head...

List some sports and then write down the components of fitness that are useful for each sport. I know it's not as fun as playing the sports, but you'll be laughing come exam time. Now, practice makes perfect and all that...

Q1 Give **two** ways that better flexibility can help a swimmer's performance. [2 marks]

Components of Fitness

Now it's time to look at <u>agility</u>, <u>balance</u>, <u>coordination</u> and <u>reaction time</u>. Just like for the components of fitness on the last two pages, you need to be able to judge their <u>importance</u> for different activities.

Agility — Control Over Your Body's Movement

1) Agility is important in any activity where you've got to run about, <u>changing direction</u> all the time, like <u>football</u> or <u>hockey</u>.

2) <u>Jumping</u> and <u>intercepting</u> a pass in <u>netball</u> or <u>basketball</u> involves a high level of <u>agility</u> too.

<u>AGILITY</u> is the ability to change <u>body position</u> or <u>direction</u> <u>quickly</u> and with <u>control</u>.

Balance — More Than Not Wobbling

<u>BALANCE</u> is the ability to <u>stay upright</u> and <u>in control</u> of any <u>movement</u>.

1) Balance requires keeping the body's <u>centre of mass</u> over a <u>base of support</u>. If you don't, you'll wobble and <u>fall over</u>.

2) Balance is <u>crucial</u> for nearly every physical activity. Any sport that involves <u>changing direction</u> quickly — like <u>football</u> or <u>basketball</u> — requires good <u>balance</u>.

3) An action that is performed with balance is more <u>efficient</u> — e.g. a <u>cyclist</u> might work on improving their balance to <u>increase</u> the speed they can go round <u>corners</u>.

Coordination — Using Body Parts Together

<u>COORDINATION</u> is the ability to use <u>two or more</u> parts of the body <u>together</u>, <u>efficiently</u> and <u>accurately</u>.

1) <u>Hand-eye coordination</u> is important in sports that require <u>precision</u>. E.g. being able to hit a ball in <u>tennis</u>, or shoot a bull's-eye in <u>archery</u>.

2) <u>Limb coordination</u> allows you to be able to <u>walk</u>, <u>run</u>, <u>dance</u>, <u>kick</u>, <u>swim</u>...

3) Coordinated movements are <u>smooth</u> and <u>efficient</u>. E.g. a <u>runner</u> with well coordinated arms and legs will be able to run <u>faster</u> than someone who is less coordinated.

4) Limb coordination is really important in sports like <u>gymnastics</u> or <u>platform diving</u>, where your performance is judged on your coordination.

Reaction Time — The Time It Takes You to React

<u>REACTION TIME</u> is the time taken to <u>move in response</u> to a <u>stimulus</u>.

1) In many sports and activities, you need to have <u>fast reactions</u>.

2) The <u>stimulus</u> you respond to could be, e.g., a <u>starter gun</u>, a <u>pass</u> in football, or a <u>serve</u> in tennis.

3) You need fast reactions to be able to <u>hit a ball</u> or <u>dodge a punch</u>. It doesn't matter how fast you can move, if you don't <u>react in time</u> you'll miss or get hit.

4) Having fast reactions can effectively give you a <u>head start</u>.

Getting away quickly at the start of a <u>sprint</u> can mean the difference between winning and losing.

Having <u>faster</u> reactions in team sports can help you <u>get away</u> from your opponents, so you can get into better playing <u>positions</u>.

Agility, Balance and Coordination — as easy as ABC...

Congratulations, you've made it. No more components of fitness to learn. You know the drill — make sure you understand what each component is and which activities it's important in. Then it's Practice Question time.

Q1 What is meant by coordination? Give an example of how coordination is important for a boxer. [2 marks]

Fitness Testing

So, you know what the components of fitness are — now you need to know how to measure them.
Read on to find out why your PE teacher made you do the stupid bleep test at 9 am in the pouring rain*.

Fitness Testing Helps Identify Strengths and Weaknesses

Fitness testing gives you data that you can analyse to help improve your fitness.

1) Fitness tests are designed to measure specific components of fitness. It's important you choose the right one for the specific component you're interested in — otherwise the test is meaningless.

2) You can use fitness testing to measure your level of fitness before starting a training programme. The data will show your strengths and weaknesses, so you can plan a personal exercise programme (see p25) that focuses on what you need to improve.

Tests need to be carried out using the same procedure each time so comparisons with previous tests are meaningful.

3) You can carry out fitness tests throughout a training programme to monitor your progress and see whether or not the training you're doing is working. This can show you where you're improving and help you set new goals.

4) The data from each of these fitness tests can be compared with national averages:

The table below shows average ratings for 16 to 19 year-olds taking the grip dynamometer test. Let's say you want to find the rating for an 18-year-old girl who scored 26 kg:

'>' means 'greater than', '<' means 'less than'.

Sex	Excellent	Good	Average	Fair	Poor
Male	> 56 kg	51-56 kg	45-50 kg	39-44 kg	< 39 kg
Female	> 36 kg	31-36 kg	25-30 kg	19-24 kg	< 19 kg

① You go down to the correct sex row.

② Then read along to find the range of numbers that includes her score.

③ Finally, go up to see which column this range is in — that gives you the rating.

So, an 18-year-old girl who scored 26 kg on the grip dynamometer test has average grip strength for her sex.

You Can Test Your Cardiovascular Endurance...

You might know this one as the 'bleep test', but use its proper name in the exam.

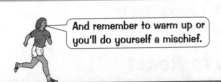

And remember to warm up or you'll do yourself a mischief.

COOPER 12-MINUTE RUN/WALK TEST

Equipment needed: stopwatch and a 400 m track.

1) Run round a track as many times as you can in 12 minutes (or walk if you get too tired to run).

2) The distance you run/walk is recorded in metres. The further it is, the better your cardiovascular endurance.

MULTI-STAGE FITNESS TEST (MSFT)

Equipment needed: tape measure, cones, multi-stage fitness test recording and some speakers to play it through.

1) A recording of a series of timed bleeps is played. You have to run 'shuttles' between two lines, 20 metres apart, starting on the first bleep. *BLEEP!!!*

2) Your foot must be on or over the next line when the next bleep sounds.

3) The time between the bleeps gets shorter as you go through the difficulty levels, so you have to run faster.

4) If you miss a bleep, you are allowed two further bleeps to catch up. If you miss three bleeps in a row, the level and number of shuttles completed are noted as your final score.

5) The higher the level and number of shuttles completed, the better your cardiovascular endurance.

I have a new revision workout for you — number crunches...

These tests are both for cardiovascular endurance. The equipment you have available might decide which you do.

Q1 Give **two** ways that data from the multi-stage fitness test could be used by an athlete training for a marathon.

[2 marks]

*Not that I'm still bitter about it or anything.

Fitness Testing

To remember the names of these fitness tests, think about the <u>action</u> involved — for <u>speed</u> you <u>sprint</u>, for <u>agility</u> you <u>run changing direction</u>, and for <u>balance</u> you <u>stand on one leg</u>... like a stork.

These Tests are for *Muscular Strength and Endurance...*

GRIP STRENGTH DYNAMOMETER TEST

<u>Equipment</u> needed: a dynamometer.

1) A <u>dynamometer</u> is a device used to measure <u>grip strength</u> — the strength in the <u>hand</u> and <u>forearm</u>.

2) You <u>grip</u> as hard as you can for about <u>five seconds</u> and <u>record</u> your reading in <u>kilograms</u>.

3) Usually, you do this <u>three</u> times and take your <u>best score</u> — the <u>higher</u> the score, the <u>stronger</u> your grip.

ONE REPETITION MAXIMUM (1RM) — MAXIMAL STRENGTH

<u>Equipment</u> needed: gym weight equipment.

1) The aim here is to find the <u>heaviest weight</u> you can <u>lift safely</u> using a particular <u>muscle group</u>. The <u>heavier</u> this weight, the <u>stronger</u> the <u>muscle group</u>.

2) <u>Start</u> with a <u>weight</u> you know you <u>can lift</u>. Once you <u>successfully</u> lift it, <u>rest</u> for a few minutes <u>before</u> trying something heavier.

3) <u>Increase</u> the weight you attempt in <u>small steps</u> until you reach a weight with which you <u>can't complete</u> a <u>single lift</u>. The <u>last</u> weight you managed to <u>successfully lift</u> is your <u>one repetition maximum</u> (or your <u>one rep max</u>).

SIT-UP AND PRESS-UP TESTS — MUSCULAR ENDURANCE

<u>Equipment</u> needed: stopwatch and a non-slip surface.

'Sit-ups' are sometimes called '<u>abdominal curls</u>'.

1001... 1002... 1003...

1) You just do <u>as many</u> sit-ups or press-ups <u>as you can</u> in a minute.

2) Your <u>result</u> is a <u>number</u> of sit-ups or press-ups — the <u>higher</u> the number, the <u>better</u> your endurance.

3) <u>Sit-ups</u> test your <u>abdominal</u> muscles' endurance, <u>press-ups</u> test your <u>upper body's</u> endurance.

Test your *Speed and Agility by Sprinting and Running...*

30 m SPRINT TEST — SPEED

<u>Equipment</u> needed: stopwatch, tape measure and cones.

1) Run the 30 m <u>as fast as you can</u> and record your time in <u>seconds</u>. The <u>shorter the time</u>, the <u>quicker</u> you are.

2) The sprint test can be done over <u>different distances</u>, e.g. 50 m is often used.

ILLINOIS AGILITY RUN TEST — AGILITY

<u>Equipment</u> needed: stopwatch, cones and a tape measure.

1) Set out a <u>course</u> using cones like this.

2) Start <u>lying face down</u> at the start cone. When a start whistle blows, run around the course as fast as you can.

3) The course is set up so you have to constantly <u>change direction</u>. The <u>shorter the time</u> (in seconds) it takes you to complete the course, the <u>more agile</u> you are.

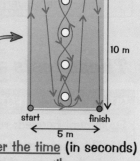

10 m

start   finish

5 m

You can test your *Balance by, erm... Balancing...*

Cheat!

THE STORK STAND TEST

<u>Equipment</u> needed: stopwatch.

1) <u>Stand</u> on your <u>best leg</u> with your other foot touching your knee and your hands on your hips.

2) Raise your heel to stand on your <u>toes</u> and <u>time how long</u> you can hold the position for in <u>seconds</u>. The test <u>finishes</u> if your heel touches the <u>ground</u>, or your other foot or hands move.

3) You usually take the <u>best</u> of three times in <u>seconds</u> — the longer your time, the <u>better</u> your <u>balance</u>.

'Another French pancake?' — *'No ta, I'm at my one crêpe max'...*

To remember which component of fitness is measured by which test, think about the action you're doing. If you're generating lots of force at once, it's testing strength, but if you're repeating a strength action, it's testing endurance.

Q1   Identify the component of fitness that a grip dynamometer test measures.   [1 mark]

Fitness Testing

Oh my, these tests just keep on coming. A load more for you to learn here, all in pretty coloured boxes...

The Ruler Drop Test is for Reaction Time...

REACTION TIME RULER DROP TEST

Equipment needed: ruler.

1) Get a friend to hold a ruler vertically between your thumb and first finger. The 0 cm mark on the ruler should be in line with the top of your thumb.

2) Your friend drops the ruler — you have to try and catch it as soon as you see it drop.

3) Read off the distance the ruler fell before you managed to catch it.

4) The slower your reactions, the longer it takes you to catch the ruler, so the further up the ruler you'll catch it. This means the smaller the distance recorded, the quicker your reaction time.

You can Test your Power by Jumping...

STANDING JUMP TEST

Equipment needed: long jump pit and a tape measure.

1) Place your feet over the edge of the pit. Then jump as far forward as possible without a run-up (you can still swing your arms to help). You have to land on both feet.

2) The distance you jump is measured in centimetres — the further you jump the more powerful your leg muscles are.

VERTICAL JUMP TEST

Equipment needed: chalk, tape measure and a wall.

1) Put chalk on your fingertips and stand side-on to a wall.

2) Raise the arm that's nearest the wall and mark the highest point you can reach.

3) Still standing side-on to the wall, jump and mark the wall as high up as you can.

4) Measure between the marks in centimetres. The larger the distance, the more powerful your leg muscles are.

These tests are for Flexibility and Coordination...

SIT AND REACH TEST — FLEXIBILITY

Equipment needed: ruler or tape measure and a box.

1) This test measures flexibility in the back and lower hamstrings.

2) You sit on the floor with your legs straight out in front of you and a box flat against your feet.

3) You then reach as far forward as you can and an assistant measures the distance reached in centimetres — the further you can reach, the more flexible your back and hamstrings are.

4) The distance reached can be measured in different ways — usually it's how many centimetres past your toes that you manage to reach.

WALL THROW TEST — COORDINATION

Equipment needed: stopwatch, a ball and a wall.

1) This tests hand-eye coordination.

2) Start by standing 2 m away from a wall.

3) Throw a ball underarm from your right hand against the wall and catch it in your left hand — then throw it underarm from your left hand against the wall and catch it in your right hand. You repeat this for 30 seconds and count the number of catches.

4) The more successful catches you make, the better your coordination.

Sit and reach for a biscuit test — now we're talking...

You made it — no more fitness tests to learn. Before you get carried away celebrating, it's Practice Question time.

Q1   Compare the suitability of the standing and vertical jump tests for a triple jumper.   [2 marks]

Principles of Training

Training isn't just about running for as long as possible, or lifting the heaviest weights you can.
There's much more to it than that — you need to know how training is matched to different people.

Train to Improve Your Health, Fitness or Performance

1) You need to be able to use the four principles of training below to make your own personal exercise (or training) programmes.

Health is a state of physical, mental and emotional well-being.

2) A personal exercise programme is designed to improve whatever you want it to improve — it could be your general health and fitness, or a particular component of fitness that will improve your performance in a sport or activity.

You will probably have completed a personal exercise programme as part of your course...

3) Different training methods involve different types of exercise and are designed to improve different components of fitness.

4) So you need to choose the right training method. Some key factors to consider will be:

For example, you might want to improve your spike in volleyball.

What area of your sport or activity you want to improve. You'll need to think about which components of fitness are involved, and which parts of the body too.

What level of fitness you are currently at — you can use fitness testing to find this out. Some methods of training may be too demanding if you are unfit. With any training method, if you're really unfit you'll want to start easy and build up the intensity slowly.

What facilities and equipment you have access to. Some training methods involve lots of specialist equipment and some will also need lots of indoor space.

The Four Principles of Training

To get the most out of your training, you need to follow these four principles:

SPECIFICITY — matching training to the activity and to the person.

Make sure you're training using the muscles and actions you want to improve — e.g. a cyclist would be better off improving their muscular endurance on an exercise bike than on a treadmill. You should also match the intensity of your training to individual needs — if someone's dead unfit, don't start them with a 5-mile swim.

PROGRESSION — gradually increasing the level of training.

This needs to be a gradual process to allow your body time to adapt. If you try to do too much too quickly, you can end up getting injured.

OVERLOAD — the only way to get fitter is to work your body harder than it normally would.

To overload, you can increase the frequency, intensity, or time spent training (see next page).

REVERSIBILITY — any fitness improvement or body adaptation caused by training will gradually reverse and be lost when you stop training.

Unfortunately, it takes longer to gain fitness than to lose fitness.

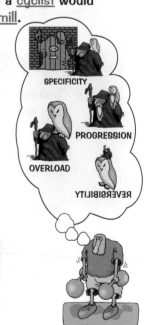

If only the fifth principle of training was Tea...

Make sure you know what all four of the principles of training mean. You could even apply them to your revision — you've got to do the right subject, go from easy to hard, do more work than normal...but don't forget it all later.

Q1 Give **one** way that a rower could apply specificity to their training. Explain your answer. [2 marks]

Principles of Training

The best training programmes aren't just thrown together — they have to be carefully planned. Part of this planning is leaving enough time for rest and recovery, so your body has time to adapt to the training.

Training Programmes can be Planned using FITT

Frequency, Intensity and Time are all part of making sure you overload while you're training.

F = FREQUENCY of training — how often you should exercise.

You can overload by increasing how often you exercise, e.g. gradually increasing the number of training sessions. You need to make sure you leave enough time between sessions to recover though (see below).

This is too intense...

I = INTENSITY of training — how hard you should exercise.

You can overload by gradually increasing the intensity of your exercise — e.g. lifting heavier weights. How intensely you train depends on the type of fitness you want to improve (see next page) and your level of fitness — someone who hasn't trained for a while should start at a low intensity and gradually increase it.

I've been hula-hooping for fifty years.

T = TIME spent training — how long you should exercise for.

You can overload by gradually increasing the time you spend on a certain exercise or by increasing the overall time spent exercising — e.g. making training sessions five minutes longer each week.

T = TYPE of training — what exercises and methods of training you should use.

You need to match the type of exercise and method of training to what it is you're training for — e.g. if you want to improve cardiovascular endurance, you need to do exercise that uses lots of muscles, like running or cycling, and you should select an appropriate method of training, e.g. continuous training (see p27). Varying the type of exercise also helps stop training becoming boring and reduces stress on tissues and joints.

All training programmes need to be constantly monitored to make sure that the activities are still producing overload. As you get fitter your personal exercise programme will need to change to keep improving your fitness.

Your Body Adapts During Rest and Recovery

I think I might have overdone it.

1) Training makes your body change to cope with the increased exercise. This means you get fitter.

2) These adaptations take place during rest and recovery, so it's vital you allow enough time between training sessions for the body to adapt.

3) It's also important that you allow enough recovery time between workouts to avoid overtraining. Overtraining is when you don't rest enough — it can cause injury by not giving your body enough time to recover from the last training session and repair any damage.

4) When you're training, you need to balance your recovery time with the effects of reversibility.

5) If you rest for too long, you'll lose most of the benefits of having done the training in the first place. If you don't rest enough, you could injure yourself through overtraining.

6) If you get injured, not only have you got to wait for your injury to heal, but thanks to reversibility, your fitness will start to decrease while you do. It doesn't seem fair really...

Someone's been really creative with these acronyms...

Want to be fit? Use **FITT** — Frequency, Intensity, Time and Type. And remember that recovery time is part of training too, because your body needs time to adapt and repair itself. Now, time for another Practice Question...

Q1 Discuss the importance of considering frequency when planning a training programme. [2 mark]

Training Methods

Next up, <u>training methods</u>. Remember, you have to match the <u>type</u> of training with what you are training for.

Continuous Training Means No Resting

1) <u>Continuous training</u> involves exercising at a <u>steady</u>, <u>constant rate</u> — doing aerobic activities like <u>running</u> or <u>cycling</u> for at least 20 minutes with <u>no breaks</u>.

2) It improves <u>cardiovascular endurance</u> and <u>muscular endurance</u> so it's good training for <u>aerobic</u> activities like <u>long-distance running</u>.

3) Continuous training leads to <u>cardiovascular adaptations</u> — your heart gets <u>bigger</u> and <u>stronger</u> (p17).

4) <u>Overload</u> is achieved by increasing the <u>duration</u>, <u>distance</u>, <u>speed</u> or <u>frequency</u>.

ADVANTAGES:
- It's <u>easy</u> to do — going for a run doesn't require <u>specialist equipment</u>.
- <u>Not resting</u> helps <u>prepare</u> for sports where you have to play for long periods of time <u>without a break</u>.

After six years of continuous training, surely I deserve a rest...

DISADVANTAGES:
- It only involves <u>aerobic</u> activity so doesn't improve <u>anaerobic fitness</u>.
- It can become <u>boring</u> doing one exercise at a constant rate.

Fartlek Training is all about Changes of Speed

1) Fartlek training is a type of continuous training, but it involves changes in the <u>intensity</u> of the exercise over <u>different intervals</u> — e.g. by changing the <u>speed</u> or the <u>terrain</u> (type or steepness of the ground).

For example, part of a fartlek run could be to <u>sprint</u> for <u>10 seconds</u>, then <u>jog</u> for <u>20 seconds</u> (repeated for 4 minutes), followed by <u>running uphill</u> for <u>2 minutes</u>.

2) It's great for <u>cardiovascular endurance</u> and <u>muscular endurance</u> and also helps to improve <u>speed</u>.

3) You can include a <u>mix</u> of <u>aerobic</u> and <u>anaerobic</u> activity (see p13), so it's good training for sports that need <u>different paces</u>, like hockey and rugby.

4) <u>Overload</u> is achieved by increasing the <u>times</u> or <u>speeds</u> of each bit, or the terrain <u>difficulty</u> (e.g. running uphill).

ADVANTAGE:
- It's very <u>adaptable</u>, so you can easily <u>tailor</u> training to suit different <u>sports</u> and different <u>levels of fitness</u>.

DISADVANTAGE:
- Frequent changes to intensity can mean that training <u>lacks structure</u> — this makes it easy to <u>skip</u> the hard bits and tough to <u>monitor</u> progress.

Interval Training uses Fixed Patterns of Exercise

1) Interval training uses <u>fixed patterns</u> of periods of <u>high-intensity</u> exercise and either <u>low-intensity</u> exercise or <u>rest</u>. It has a strict <u>structure</u>.

2) By combining high- and low-intensity work, interval training allows you to improve both <u>cardiovascular endurance</u> and <u>anaerobic fitness</u>. The <u>high-intensity</u> periods can also improve <u>speed</u>.

3) It's great training for sports where you have to <u>move continuously</u> (aerobic), then have <u>sudden spurts</u> of <u>fast</u> movement (anaerobic) — like <u>rugby</u> or <u>water polo</u>.

4) To <u>overload</u> you have to increase the <u>proportion of time</u> spent on the <u>high-intensity</u> exercise, or the <u>overall intensity</u> — e.g. run faster.

ADVANTAGE:
- It's <u>easily adapted</u> to improve <u>aerobic</u> or <u>anaerobic</u> fitness by changing the <u>intensity</u> and <u>length</u> of <u>work</u> and <u>recovery</u> periods.

DISADVANTAGE:
- Interval training is <u>exhausting</u>. This can make it difficult to carry on <u>pushing</u> yourself.

Nige's interval training: run for 1 minute, bathe for 30 minutes, and repeat...

Fartlek training — .... (Add your own joke.)

Once you're done admiring your own wit, there's an Exam Practice Question with your name on it...

Q1   Assess whether continuous training is better training for a marathon or for a 100 m sprint.   [4 marks]

Training Methods

Weight training helps you to get stronger. Circuit training lets you do lots of different exercises in one go.

Weight Training works on your Muscles

Weight training means using your muscles against a resistance. You can use weights, elastic ropes or your own body weight (like in a pull-up or press-up) as the resistance.

Improving your strength will also help increase your power.

1) Weight training can be used to develop both strength and muscular endurance.

2) It's anaerobic training, so is good for improving performance in anaerobic activities like sprinting.

3) Increasing strength/power means you can hit or kick something harder (hockey, football), throw further (javelin, discus), sprint faster, out-muscle opposition (judo), etc.

You can train by contracting your muscles to create movement. Each completed movement is called a 'rep' (repetition), and a group of reps is called a 'set'.

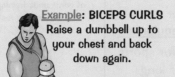
Example: BICEPS CURLS
Raise a dumbbell up to your chest and back down again.

See p23 for how to find your one rep max.

- To increase muscular endurance, you use low weight (below 70% of your one rep max) but a high number of reps — approximately three sets of 12-15 reps. To overload, gradually increase the number of reps.

- To increase strength you use high weight (above 70% of your one rep max) but a low number of reps — approximately three sets of 4-8 reps. To overload, gradually increase the weight — but decrease the reps to avoid injury.

- It's important you use the correct lifting technique to prevent injury and lift an appropriate weight to avoid over training.

ADVANTAGES:
- It's easily adapted to suit different sports — you can focus on the relevant muscles.
- Many of the exercises (press-ups, sit-ups, etc.) require little or no equipment.

DISADVANTAGES:
- It puts muscles under high stress levels, so can leave them very sore afterwards.
- If your weightlifting technique is poor, it can be dangerous. Also, some lifts require an assistant.

The assistant is called a 'spotter'.

Circuit Training Uses Loads of Different Exercises

Each circuit has between 6 and 10 'stations' in it. At each station you do a specific exercise for a set amount of time before moving on to the next station.

1) A circuit's stations can work on aerobic or anaerobic fitness — e.g. star jumps for cardiovascular endurance, tricep dips for strength, shuttle runs for speed, etc.

2) You're allowed a short rest between stations. An active rest, e.g. jogging instead of stopping exercising, will improve cardiovascular endurance.

3) Overload is achieved by doing more repetitions at each station, completing the circuit more quickly, resting less between stations, or by repeating the circuit.

ADVANTAGES:
- Because you design the circuit, you can match circuit training to an individual and any component of fitness — e.g. you can improve muscular endurance, strength, cardiovascular endurance... anything you want really.

DISADVANTAGE:
- It takes a long time to set up and requires loads of equipment and space.

- Also, the variety keeps the training interesting.

I prefer wait training myself — far less strenuous...

Make sure that you understand how weight training can help with muscular endurance and strength.
For endurance do low weight, high reps. For strength do high weight, low reps. Keep saying it over and over...

Q1   Describe how an athlete can train using weights to improve their strength.   [2 marks]

Training Methods

Plyometrics helps make you more powerful. High-intensity interval training (HIIT) improves your cardiovascular endurance and anaerobic fitness using short, intense bursts of exercise.

Plyometric Training Improves Power

Loads of sports require explosive strength and power (see p19-20), e.g. for fast sprinting starts, or sports where you need to jump high, like basketball or volleyball. You can train muscular power using plyometrics.

1) When muscles 'contract' to give movement, they either shorten or lengthen.

2) If a muscle lengthens just before it shortens, it can help to generate power. When a muscle gets stretched and lengthens, extra energy is stored in the muscle (like storing energy in an elastic band by stretching it). This extra energy means the muscle can generate a greater force when it shortens.

3) The extra energy doesn't last very long though. So, the quicker your muscles can move between the lengthening and shortening phases, the more powerful the movement will be.

4) Plyometric training improves the speed you can switch between the two phases, so it improves your power. It's anaerobic exercise and often involves jumping.

Depth jumps are a form of plyometric training. They improve the power of your quadriceps and increase how high you can jump. You drop off a box then quickly jump into the air. The first stage lengthens your quadriceps as you land and squat, the second stage shortens them as you jump.

ADVANTAGE:
- It's the only form of training that directly improves your power.

DISADVANTAGE:
- It's very demanding on the muscles used — you need to be very fit to do it, otherwise you'll get injured.

HIIT Improves Cardiovascular Endurance

1) High-intensity interval training (HIIT) is a form of interval training where you use maximum effort for the high-intensity bits, and an active, low-intensity rest period.

2) The high-intensity bits are done at over 70% of your maximum possible effort. These last for short periods of time so that you can push yourself hard. Low-intensity bits are 50% or less of your maximum effort and should last around twice as long as high-intensity stages.

3) So you might do HIIT by sprinting for 20 seconds, then jogging for 40 seconds, then sprinting again.

4) The short, high-intensity bursts allows you to improve cardiovascular endurance, anaerobic fitness, strength and speed. There is also some evidence that HIIT can have health benefits.

5) To overload you have to increase the intensity of the high-intensity exercise — e.g. run faster.

ADVANTAGES:
- HIIT workouts tend to be short — so they're good for people who don't have much time.
- It can be effective to help to lose fat without losing muscle.
- It can be easily adapted to different sports.

DISADVANTAGE:
- Interval training can be very tiring and it can be hard to find the motivation to push to maximum effort.

Aerobike training

I tried high-intensity training once — I definitely HIIT the wall...

Both the training methods covered on this page are a bit tricky — take your time and make sure you understand what components of fitness they help with, and what type of performer uses them. Time for a Practice Question...

Q1 Explain why a basketball player would train using plyometrics. [2 marks]

Warming Up and Cooling Down

Warming up before exercise and cooling down afterwards are vital — they have tons of benefits.

Before Exercise you should always Warm Up...

A warm-up gets your body ready for exercise by gradually increasing your work rate. It should involve:

1) Pulse raising — light exercise increases your heart rate and gets blood flowing to the muscles.
   - This raises your body temperature and warms up muscles, ligaments and tendons so they can move more freely and are less likely to get injured. Warmer muscles can also contract more quickly.
   - It also helps to ease your body into exercising by gradually increasing the exercise intensity, and it increases the oxygen supply to the muscles.

2) Mobility exercises — these move joints through their full range of motion. They should focus on the movements you will use in the activity — e.g. shoulder circles before playing tennis, or hip circles before running.

Mobility exercises and stretching help to increase the range of movements of your muscles and joints, which will help you perform better and avoid injury.

3) Stretching — Static stretching is done by gradually stretching a muscle and then holding the position. However, it's best to use dynamic stretching, e.g. lunges, high kicks.

4) Dynamic movements involve quick movements, e.g. agility ladder exercises. They work on agility and the speed of muscle contraction.

5) Skill rehearsal — e.g. practice shots in netball, throwing and catching in rounders, etc.
   - This prepares the muscles that will be used in the activity, so they perform better.
   - It also helps with your mental preparation, as it focuses you on the activity and gets you "in the zone".

You could also use mental preparation techniques so you're calm, confident and focused (see page 44).

...And Afterwards you should Cool Down

A cool-down helps transition your body back to a resting state after exercise. It does this by gradually decreasing the intensity of work to control your return to resting levels. It should involve:

LOW-INTENSITY EXERCISE like jogging to keep the heart and lungs working harder than normal. The intensity is gradually reduced (e.g. going from a jog to walking).
- Gradually reducing the intensity allow your heart rate, breathing rate and body temperature to decrease gradually back to their resting levels.
- Gradually reducing your heart rate and breathing rate means that you can continue taking in more oxygen to help get rid of the lactic acid and other waste products in your muscles (repaying the oxygen debt — see p14). It also helps you to remove the extra carbon dioxide in your blood.
- It keeps the blood flowing back from the muscles, so stops blood pooling in the legs and arms — blood pooling can cause dizziness and even fainting.

STRETCHING the muscles that have been used in the activity to speed up recovery and improve flexibility.
- Stretching while the muscles are warm helps to improve flexibility — in particular using static or PNF stretches. PNF stretches involve contracting the muscle you are stretching to increase mobility gains.
- It may also help to prevent muscle stiffness and delayed onset of muscle soreness (DOMS).

Putting on a big jumper — my favourite way to warm up...

Warming up is especially important for more intense, anaerobic activities, where it's easy to get an injury.

Q1* Evaluate the importance of a pre-match warm-up in helping a hockey player to avoid injury. [6 marks]

Preventing Injuries

With any physical activity there's always a risk of injury. You need to know how to make it as safe as possible.

Do these Things to Minimise the Risk of Injury...

There are lots of different things you can do to prevent injuries when doing exercise. This includes checking that the equipment you're using is in good condition and that you're applying the Principles of Training (see p25-26).

USE THE CORRECT CLOTHING/FOOTWEAR

- Make sure you're not wearing anything that could get caught (e.g. jewellery, watches).
- Wear suitable footwear — e.g. wearing studded football boots or spiked running shoes can make you less likely to slip and injure yourself.

WARMING UP AND COOLING DOWN

- See page 30 for how to warm up and cool down properly...
- Warming up prepares your muscles and joints for the movements that will happen during exercise.
- Cooling down can help to prevent muscle stiffness and soreness.

COMPETE AT THE APPROPRIATE LEVEL

- You should exercise with people at a similar level to yourself, so you don't overdo it — e.g. join a running club which runs at a similar pace to yourself.
- You need to compete in the right age range too — e.g. a 10-year-old shouldn't play rugby with adults.

USE PERSONAL PROTECTIVE EQUIPMENT

- Personal protective equipment (PPE) is used to prevent injuries.
- For example, you should wear a helmet when cycling, to protect your head from injuries if you crash or fall over.
- In contact sports, gumshields prevent damage to the teeth and mouth.

LIFT AND CARRY EQUIPMENT SAFELY

- Make sure that you use the correct technique to lift and carry things.
- This involves bending your knees rather than your back.
- There might be special rules for moving certain pieces of equipment — follow them.

Know the Hazards in Different Places

Depending on where you're doing exercise or sport, there can be different hazards (things that risk causing injury) that you need to look out for. Once you have checked for hazards, you can put appropriate safety measures in place. For example:

1) SPORTS HALL — slippery floors, badly stored equipment, damaged equipment and trip hazards (such as dividing nets) can all pose risks. You should make sure that the floors and equipment are properly maintained, things are put away correctly and that people are aware of trip hazards.

2) FITNESS CENTRE — using weights incorrectly (or using a weight that is too heavy) can cause injury. It's important to make sure that health and safety instructions are given to users. It might also be necessary to provide supervision on some equipment.

3) PLAYING FIELD — Any holes and lumps in the grass could cause tripping and ankle injuries. The playing field should also be checked for rubbish, such as broken glass.

4) ARTIFICIAL OUTDOOR AREA — artificial grass can cause injuries from falls if it wrinkles — this can be prevented by applying infill sand to the surface. Any equipment should also be checked to ensure that it's not damaged.

5) SWIMMING POOL — water is a hazard that can lead to drowning so there need to be depth signs and lifeguards. Having rules (e.g. no running or dive bombing) also minimises risk.

All this talk of injuries is making my brain hurt...

You need to be able to apply these ways of preventing injury to different activities, so think about the actions involved and also where the activity takes place. Now, time for an Exam Practice Question to check you've got it.

Q1 Explain **one** way that a rugby player can avoid injury during a match. [1 mark]

Revision Questions for Section Three

So, it turns out there's more to <u>physical training</u> than montages, slow motion and cheesy power ballads...
- Try these questions and <u>tick off each one</u> when you <u>get it right</u>.
- When you've done <u>all the questions</u> for a topic and are <u>completely happy</u> with it, tick off the topic.
- The answers can all be found by <u>looking back over pages 19 to 31</u>.

<u>Components of Fitness (p19-21)</u> ☑

1) What is cardiovascular endurance? ☑
2) Give an example of a sport where muscular endurance is important. ☑
3) What is power? Give an example of when power would be needed in golf. ☑
4) Define agility. Give a practical example of how it is important for an athlete. ☑
5) Describe coordination. How does having good coordination help a sprinter? ☑

<u>Fitness Testing (p22-24)</u> ☑

6) How would you use a fitness test to measure progress during a training programme? ☑
7) Describe the Cooper 12-minute run test. Which component of fitness does it measure? ☑
8) Outline a fitness test that measures: a) muscular endurance, b) speed, c) agility, d) power. ☑
9) Which component of fitness does the sit and reach test measure? ☑

<u>Principles of Training (p25-26)</u> ☑

10) Name four important principles of training. ☑
11) Give three ways that overload can be achieved in training. ☑
12) What does each letter in **FITT** mean? ☑

<u>Training Methods (p27-29)</u> ☑

13) Does continuous training improve anaerobic fitness? ☑
14) Describe the fartlek training method. Give an advantage and a disadvantage. ☑
15) How is overload achieved in circuit training? ☑
16) Which component of fitness does plyometric training improve? ☑
17) Explain **HIIT** and give an example of how it could be done. ☑

<u>Warming up and Cooling Down (p30)</u> ☑

18) Why does raising the heart rate in a warm up help prepare for exercise? ☑
19) Outline two other benefits of warming up. ☑
20) What should you do in a cool down? ☑
21) Explain two benefits of cooling down. ☑

<u>Preventing Injuries (p31)</u> ☑

22) Explain how using the correct footwear can help to prevent injuries. ☑
23) Why is it important to compete at an appropriate level when playing sport? ☑
24) Give two hazards that could be found in a sports hall. ☑
25) How could injuries be prevented in a fitness centre? ☑

Influences on Participation

Participation rates are how many people take part in sport or other physical activities.

> According to Sport England research, the sports with the most adult participants in England in 2015/2016 were swimming, athletics (which includes running), cycling and football.
> A reason for this may be that more people have the opportunity to participate in these sports. For example, there are more people with access to a swimming pool than to a snowsports centre.

Whether you participate in sport, and the type of sport you play, can be affected by many different factors...

The Media Influences Participation in Sport

There's more on the effect of media on sport on p37.

The media can inspire people to take part in sports and provide role models.

1) When big sporting events are in the media, people are often encouraged to have a go themselves. For example, participation in sport in England peaked at the time of the London 2012 Olympics. Also, tennis centres see a big rise in the number of people booking courts when Wimbledon is on the TV.

2) People who excel in their sport can become role models for their sport and inspire people to be like them. This encourages more people to participate in their sport.

Your Gender may Influence whether you do an Activity

Although things are getting better, there's still a real gender divide in participation. Surveys carried out by Sport England show that, overall, fewer women participate regularly in sport than men.

1) This may be because many women's events have a lower profile than men's, as they get less media coverage. This has meant that in many sports there are fewer female role models to inspire younger generations to take up the sport.

2) Less media coverage also means there is less sponsorship available for women's sport, meaning there are fewer opportunities and less money for women to do sport at a high level.

3) Gender tagging — outdated attitudes about some things being "women's activities" and others being "men's activities" — might also affect what sports you decide to take up.

4) This includes gender stereotypes about it 'not being feminine' to get sweaty or muddy, or to play sports where you need aggression. Similarly, stereotypes about masculinity may also mean boys are expected to play more aggressive sports or mocked for enjoying activities seen as less 'manly'.

Ethnicity and Religion can have an Effect too

1) Religious and cultural beliefs and ethnicity can influence the physical activity people do.

> E.g. many Muslim women keep their bodies covered up. This may mean they're less likely to participate in activities such as swimming because of the clothing that's expected to be worn.

2) Religious festivals and days may impact on when you can play sport. For example, some Christians won't play sport on a Sunday because it's the Sabbath, so could not join a Sunday league team.

3) Racism and racial abuse can be a problem in sport. Campaigns against racism, such as the Let's Kick Racism Out Of Football campaign, have helped to raise awareness of the problem. Also, punishments for players and fans who are racist are now much more severe than they used to be.

4) Governing bodies have also tried to help create more positive role models to inspire and engage younger generations to participate.

5) Policies like the 'Rooney Rule' in American football, which says that teams must interview at least one ethnic minority candidate for any head coaching job, are also helping to create more opportunities.

That was such a good somersault — you're my roll model...

Ethnicity and gender shouldn't affect participation in sport, but unfortunately they do. The reasons why some groups have lower participation rates are not straightforward. There are usually lots of factors that come into play.

Q1   Suggest **one** reason why fewer women than men participate in sport.   [1 mark]

Influences on Participation

Another page of <u>influences on participation</u> — so many influences, so little time...

Disability can Influence how Active you are

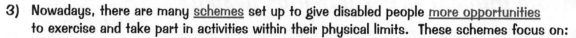

1) Having a <u>disability</u> can limit the physical activities you can do. Studies show that participation rates for disabled people are <u>lower</u> than they are for non-disabled people.

2) The <u>opportunities</u> in sport and <u>access to sporting facilities</u> for disabled people used to be few and far between.

3) Nowadays, there are many <u>schemes</u> set up to give disabled people <u>more opportunities</u> to exercise and take part in activities within their physical limits. These schemes focus on:

- <u>Adapting</u> sports so that they're more <u>accessible</u> for disabled people — e.g. basketball or handcycling.
- <u>Creating new sports</u> specifically for disabled people — like boccia (a game like bowls that can be played from a wheelchair) and goalball (a game like handball that <u>visually impaired</u> people can play).
- <u>Including</u> disabled people in activities alongside non-disabled people. This helps to <u>challenge stereotypes</u> about disabled people as well as giving disabled people the <u>opportunity</u> to enjoy a <u>wide range</u> of activities.

4) Disabled sporting events are now given a lot more <u>media coverage</u> than they once were. The Paralympic Games now get extensive <u>media coverage</u>, like the Olympics.

5) This media coverage is helping to <u>change people's attitudes</u> towards disability and sport.

6) It's also helping create many more <u>disabled role models</u> (like <u>Dame Tanni Grey-Thompson</u> and <u>Ellie Simmonds</u>), which encourages more disabled people to get active.

Your Disposable Income also has an Effect...

<u>Disposable income</u> is the money you have <u>left to spend</u> after paying for essentials, e.g. bills and food. People with <u>less disposable income</u> are <u>less likely</u> to regularly take part in sport. The <u>kinds</u> of activities people do can also be affected by how much money they can <u>afford</u> to spend.

1) Most sports cost <u>money</u>, e.g. leisure centres and gyms usually charge. <u>Travelling</u> to facilities can also cost money.

2) Lots of sports — like <u>horse riding</u>, <u>sailing</u> and even <u>cycling</u> — require specialist <u>equipment</u> and <u>clothing</u>. This can be very <u>expensive</u>.

...and so do Work and Family Commitments

1) Playing sport requires a lot of <u>free time</u>. If you <u>work long hours</u>, or have <u>family commitments</u> like caring for children, you might just <u>not</u> have the <u>time</u>.

2) If you work <u>irregular hours</u> it can be hard to join clubs that meet in the evenings or at weekends.

Family Influences the Activities you do

1) Parents might <u>encourage</u> their children to take up sports, or <u>discourage</u> them. Children often need their parents to <u>pay</u> for them to take part, and to <u>take them to facilities</u>.

2) If your parents or siblings <u>play sport</u>, or are <u>interested</u> in it, you're <u>familiar</u> with sport from a young age. You may also have <u>more opportunities</u> to take part.

We're all under the influence...

You need to understand how all these factors can have an effect on participation rates and what sports people participate in. And now, treat yourself and have a pop at this Exam Practice Question...

Q1 Give **one** reason why having work or family commitments might decrease participation in sport.   [1 mark]

Influences on Participation

That's right, it's <u>another page</u> of influences on participation. Just like the rest of them, there's a bunch of facts to get your head around. So, <u>buckle up</u>, get <u>comfortable</u> and set your <u>brain</u> to 'memorise'...

Age can Limit the Activities you can do

1) Research shows that people are <u>less likely</u> to participate in sport the <u>older</u> they get.
2) Younger people usually have <u>loads of choice</u> for physical activity. But as people get older, they're often <u>physically limited</u> in the sports they can choose. They tend to do <u>less strenuous</u> activities like walking or swimming. There might also be a lack of <u>suitable activities</u> available.
3) Some sports, such as <u>weightlifting</u> or <u>endurance events</u>, can potentially <u>damage</u> a <u>young person's</u> body. Competitions in such activities often have a <u>minimum age restriction</u>.
4) Young people often have more <u>spare time</u> to do sport. As people get <u>older</u> and have <u>careers</u> and <u>families</u>, there's <u>less time</u> available for playing sport.

PE in Schools can have a Big Effect on Participation

Research shows that interest and involvement in sport between the ages of <u>11 and 16</u> is linked to lifelong participation. So it's no wonder that PE plays a big <u>role</u> in shaping feelings towards sport and exercise.

1) <u>PE classes</u> and <u>after-school activities</u> are a way for students to try out lots of different sports. This allows students to become <u>familiar</u> with lots of activities, which might encourage regular participation. It's really important that schools offer a <u>wide range</u> of activities, so there's something for everyone. This will <u>encourage</u> more students to <u>join in</u> and <u>enjoy</u> sport:
   - Some students are put off by PE at school because they find it <u>awkward</u> or <u>embarrassing</u>.
   - Allowing students to <u>choose</u> what activities they would like to do, and listening to students' suggestions about improving PE, can make students <u>more willing</u> to take part.
   - Some students do not enjoy the <u>competitive</u> nature of sport, so offering <u>non-competitive activities</u> in PE is a good idea — e.g. fitness classes or yoga.
2) Having a really good PE <u>teacher</u>, or sports coach at a club, can really help to <u>inspire</u> people too. The flip side of this is that a <u>bad experience</u> in PE could end up <u>putting you off</u> sports and exercise.
3) The <u>facilities</u> a school has available can <u>limit</u> what activities it can offer. Also, grimy old <u>changing rooms</u> and <u>equipment</u> can mean some students just aren't <u>inspired</u> to <u>join in</u> with PE at all.
4) In PE you should learn <u>physical literacy</u>. This means you have basic skills like <u>running</u>, <u>jumping</u>, <u>throwing</u>, <u>catching</u> and <u>swimming</u> that you can use as a starting point for learning lots of new activities and sports. These skills allow you to go on and <u>take part</u> in physical activity <u>throughout</u> your life.

Even the Environment has an Effect

This was a terrible idea...

1) If you live nowhere near <u>mountains</u> and <u>snow</u>, the opportunities to compete in many <u>winter sports</u> will be <u>few and far between</u>.*
2) In very hot and very cold climates, it might not be possible to be <u>outside</u> and <u>active</u> for long periods of time, which can affect participation in sports.
3) <u>Pollution levels</u> can force people to remain <u>indoors</u>, making it <u>harder</u> to participate in a lot of sports.
4) The <u>layout</u> of a <u>city</u> can dramatically affect participation in <u>running</u>, <u>cycling</u> and other <u>outdoor activities</u> — without <u>pavements</u>, <u>cycle lanes</u> and <u>green spaces</u> like parks, there is nowhere to do these things.
5) Really <u>mountainous</u> regions may struggle to have <u>flat areas</u> for creating <u>pitches</u>, so participation in many team sports can be difficult.

*No one told the Jamaican bobsleigh team this.

I keep dropping my books — I think I'm physically illiterate...

All these influences work together to shape our attitude towards physical activity — make sure to get 'em learned...

Q1 Give **two** ways that schools can encourage students to enjoy sport and physical activity. [2 marks]

Influences on Participation

You need to know about ways of <u>improving</u> participation rates, and how to <u>interpret data</u> about participation.

Learn these *Three Strategies* for *Encouraging Participation*

There are three main ways of improving participation rates: <u>promotion</u>, <u>provision</u> and <u>access</u>:

PROMOTION

1) Participation can be <u>promoted</u> through <u>advertising campaigns</u>, e.g.:
   - Sport England's <u>This Girl Can</u> campaign, launched in 2015, <u>challenges stereotypes</u> about women in sport.
   - Public Health England's <u>Change4Life</u> campaign aims to tackle <u>obesity</u> by encouraging families to improve their <u>diet</u> and be more <u>active</u>.

2) <u>Media coverage</u> of sporting events like the Paralympics and the Women's World Cup in football can also help <u>inspire</u> participation and <u>challenge stereotypes</u>.

3) More locally, <u>clubs</u> and <u>facilities</u> can be promoted to local residents through <u>local advertising</u>, so they know what's <u>available</u> in their area.

PROVISION

1) Providing <u>facilities</u> and well-trained <u>staff</u> can help to encourage more people to take up sports and activities.

2) It's important that these facilities cater to a <u>wide range</u> of people by offering plenty of <u>variety</u> — including offering a range of activities for disabled and elderly folk.

3) Activities need to be offered at a range of <u>times</u> so that people <u>working</u> long or irregular hours have the <u>opportunity</u> to take part.

4) <u>Leisure centres</u> usually provide a wide range of classes and activities, and have trained staff and coaches to help all kinds of people be <u>active</u> and <u>healthy</u>.

5) <u>PE classes</u> and <u>clubs</u> after <u>school</u> help provide students with opportunities to participate in sport and exercise (see p35).

ACCESS

1) Having <u>access</u> to facilities can be a problem, especially in <u>rural</u> areas. Also, sometimes it can be difficult for families without a <u>car</u> to get involved in lots of sporting activities.

2) The government can help by providing good <u>public transport</u> links. Organisations like Sport England help clubs buy <u>minibuses</u> and other methods of <u>transportation</u>. Some <u>disabled</u> people may also require <u>specialist equipment</u>, like ramps, to be able to use these methods of transport.

3) Access can be improved by clubs and facilities being <u>reasonably priced</u>, so people can <u>afford</u> to use them.

You'll Need to *Interpret Data* about *Participation Rates*

In the exam, you'll need to be able to <u>analyse graphs</u> showing participation rates for different sports and activities.

1) You may get asked to <u>compare activities</u>, e.g. to say for which activity participation has <u>increased</u> or <u>decreased</u> most from one point to another.

2) The <u>bigger</u> the <u>difference</u> between these <u>two points</u>, the <u>bigger</u> the <u>increase</u> or <u>decrease</u>.

3) For example, the graph on the right shows that:
   - Participation in <u>running increased</u> more than in football or cycling from <u>07/08</u> to <u>15/16</u>.
   - Participation in <u>football decreased</u> more than in cycling or athletics from <u>11/12</u> to <u>12/13</u>.

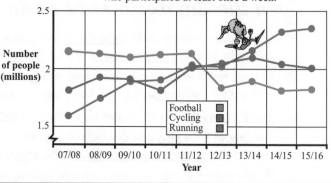

Graph showing the number of English people aged 16 or over who participated at least once a week.

Number of people (millions)

Football ■
Cycling ■
Running ■

Year
07/08 08/09 09/10 10/11 11/12 12/13 13/14 14/15 15/16

Participation — you've got to be in it to win it...

You could get a graph showing participation rates for different groups — e.g. rates for men and women. You might need to use the reasons covered on these pages to explain the differences too. Now, Practice Question time.

Q1 Using the graph above, which of these sports had the highest participation rate in 2013-14?

    A Football   **B** Cycling   **C** Running   **D** Golf   [1 mark]

Commercialisation of Sport

Lots of people are raking in cash from sport these days. This is called <u>commercialisation</u>. Here are the facts...

Commercialisation Means Making Money

1) The <u>commercialisation</u> of sport is all about <u>making money</u> from it.

2) A lot of money comes from <u>sponsorship</u> — if people are going to <u>see</u> it, companies will slap their <u>name</u> on it, whether it's a person, team, league, stand, trophy, mascot or ball. This is great <u>advertising</u> for the sponsor. As well as money, <u>sponsors</u> might also provide <u>equipment</u>, <u>clothing</u> or <u>facilities</u>.

3) Money also comes from the <u>media</u> — <u>organisations</u> involved in <u>mass communication</u> — like <u>television</u> companies, <u>radio</u> broadcasters and <u>newspapers</u>.

4) The media pay so they can <u>cover</u> the sport, which means people will <u>buy</u> their <u>newspaper</u> or <u>watch</u> their <u>TV channel</u>. Some companies sell sport on TV, or over the Internet, as a <u>subscription package</u> too.

5) Broadcasting sports on <u>television</u> and the <u>Internet</u> means it now reaches an even larger, <u>global audience</u> — this is known as the <u>globalisation of sport</u>. This all makes sponsorship even more valuable.

6) <u>Social media</u> gives <u>fans</u> new ways to interact with their favourite <u>sports stars</u> and <u>teams</u>. This keeps <u>sponsors</u> of those teams and players in the <u>public eye</u>, which <u>promotes</u> them even more.

7) Sports also make money through selling <u>tickets</u> to events, and <u>merchandise</u>.

Sport, the Media and Sponsorship are all Connected

<u>Sport</u>, <u>the media</u> and <u>sponsorship</u> have grown to <u>depend</u> on one another — this is called the '<u>golden triangle</u>'.

There are advantages and disadvantages to these relationships for the <u>sponsor</u>, the <u>sport</u>, the <u>players</u>, the <u>spectators</u> and the <u>officials</u>.

First up, the influence of the <u>media</u>:

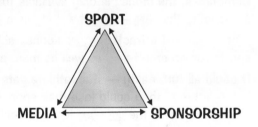

SPORT

MEDIA ◄─────► SPONSORSHIP

THE MEDIA AND SPORT

1) The media <u>pay</u> for the rights to cover sporting events, which provides <u>investment</u> for <u>sports</u> to <u>develop</u> at lower levels.

2) Media coverage makes <u>more</u> people <u>aware</u> of the sport, so more people may <u>play</u> it or watch it.

3) Media coverage of <u>elite</u> players and athletes can create <u>role models</u> who <u>inspire</u> people to play.

4) This can make <u>players</u> into superstars. But, the downside is that <u>players</u> are <u>hounded</u> by the media and their <u>private lives</u> are all over the news.

5) Also, the media can hold so much <u>power over</u> sport that they'll <u>change</u> things:
   - The <u>number</u> of games played, or the <u>timings</u> of matches, might be changed so more matches can be shown. This risks <u>injury</u> to <u>players</u> through lack of rest, and might mean <u>spectators</u> miss a game because it's not at a convenient time.
   - Also, <u>rules</u> may be changed — e.g. the <u>tiebreaker</u> set was brought into tennis to make matches shorter.

6) Being able to watch on <u>TV</u> or the <u>Internet</u>, rather than going to the game, can save <u>fans</u> money. However, fewer fans buying tickets means losses in ticket sales for <u>the sport</u> and a poorer atmosphere at the stadium for <u>spectators</u>.

7) The media's <u>analysis</u> of refereeing decisions puts <u>sports officials</u> under a lot of <u>pressure</u>.

8) Media analysis of games can also <u>educate spectators</u>, so they <u>understand</u> the sport better.

I don't write these jokes for the money — I do it for the love, man...

Get this commercialisation stuff memorised and the marks will flow like famous footballers' sponsorship deals.

Q1 Give **two** ways that media interest in a sport affects participation levels.
    For each, explain how participation is affected.   [4 marks]

Commercialisation of Sport

<u>Sponsorship</u> has a big effect on sport and everyone involved in it. You need to know its <u>upsides</u> and <u>downsides</u>.

Sponsorship Provides *Funding* in Return for *Advertising*

Sports and athletes need <u>money</u>, and they get a lot of it from <u>sponsorship</u>. The sponsors <u>aren't</u> doing it for the love of sport though — they want to <u>sell more products</u> and <u>look good</u>.

SPONSORSHIP AND SPORT

1) Sponsorship deals mean companies can associate their name with the <u>prestige</u> of successful <u>sportspeople</u> and <u>teams</u>. This is an effective form of <u>advertising</u>, which helps <u>the sponsor</u> to make more money.

2) These deals mean <u>big money</u> for sport — which can be spent on <u>development</u>, e.g. of a new stadium or facilities. This benefits the <u>players</u> and the <u>spectators</u>.

3) Sponsorship money also means <u>players</u> and <u>officials</u> can be paid good <u>wages</u>, and players can train full-time. This benefits <u>everyone</u>, because they will <u>perform</u> better.

SPONSORSHIP AND THE MEDIA

1) The more <u>media coverage</u> a sport gets, the more people <u>watch</u> it. This makes <u>sponsorship</u> more <u>valuable</u>, as it can reach a <u>larger audience</u>.

2) This increases the likelihood of sponsorship and means <u>the sport</u> and <u>players</u> can <u>demand more money</u> for their sponsorship deals.

Sponsorship Isn't All Great

1) Sometimes, the money is only available for the <u>top players</u> and teams, so benefits the <u>elite</u> — <u>not</u> the <u>sport</u> as a <u>whole</u>.

2) <u>Women's sport</u> attracts <u>far less</u> sponsorship than men's sport. This means sportswomen aren't <u>paid</u> as well as men, and often <u>can't</u> train full-time.

3) It could all turn nasty — if an athlete gets <u>injured</u>, loses their <u>form</u> or gets a <u>bad reputation</u> they could lose their sponsorship deal. <u>Bad behaviour</u> by an <u>athlete</u> reflects badly on the <u>sponsor</u> too and could <u>damage</u> the company's <u>reputation</u>.

4) Sometimes athletes have to fulfil <u>contracts</u> with their sponsor — they might have to turn up at a <u>special event</u> or appear in a <u>TV advert</u> (even if they don't want to).

5) Athletes can get into <u>trouble</u> with their sponsor if they're spotted using <u>another company's</u> products.

6) If a team really <u>needs</u> a sponsor's money, this puts the sponsor in a position of <u>power</u>. This means they can <u>influence</u> the team's playing style or team selection.

7) In some sports where there are breaks in play, <u>adverts</u> will be shown. The game won't be allowed to <u>restart</u> until the advert break is <u>finished</u>, which can be quite <u>boring</u> for <u>spectators</u> in the stadium.

Why's he playing?
His dad sponsors the team.

Some Sponsors are Inappropriate

Sponsorship brings in loads of money, but you have to be careful not to <u>promote</u> the <u>wrong</u> image, especially in <u>youth</u> sports:

1) <u>Cigarette</u> and <u>tobacco</u> companies aren't allowed to sponsor sports in the UK. This is because their products are <u>harmful</u> and <u>unhealthy</u>.

2) <u>Alcoholic drinks</u> companies are allowed to sponsor some sports, but this can be <u>bad</u> as it gives alcohol a <u>false image of health</u>. The same is true for <u>unhealthy food</u> companies.

3) Also, as sport is watched by <u>children</u>, advertising alcohol and fast food could be <u>encouraging</u> young people to <u>drink</u> or <u>eat unhealthily</u>.

CGP CGP CGP CGP (CGP — Official Sponsors of page 38)...

Make sure that you can weigh up the pros and cons of sponsorship. Try this question to check you've got it...

Q1* An elite hockey player gains sponsorship from a multinational company. Evaluate the impacts that this will have on the player. [6 marks]

Ethical Issues in Sport

This page is about good and bad <u>behaviour</u> in sport. Turns out taking your ball home if you're <u>losing</u> isn't okay.

Sportsmanship is About Being Fair and Polite

Being a good sportsperson is <u>more</u> than just playing by the rules.
You also have to show good '<u>sportsmanship</u>' (even if you lose).

> <u>Sportsmanship</u> means playing <u>fairly</u>, <u>sticking to the rules</u>
> and being <u>polite</u> and <u>respectful</u> to your opponents.

1) This means no <u>rubbing it in</u> the opposition's face if you <u>win</u>. And no going <u>off in a huff</u> if you <u>lose</u>.

2) It also means observing the <u>etiquette</u> of an activity — following <u>unwritten rules</u> and <u>conventions</u>. E.g.:

- In cricket, a batsman might choose to '<u>walk</u>' if they think they've been caught <u>out</u> — even if the umpire has <u>ruled</u> them <u>not out</u>.
- In football, players will kick the ball <u>out of play</u> if a member of the other team goes down <u>injured</u>.

Gamesmanship and Deviance — Types of Poor Behaviour

These two things are both <u>unethical</u> and go <u>against</u> the spirit of the game.
But <u>only one</u> involves actually <u>breaking the rules</u>...

> <u>Gamesmanship</u> is gaining an advantage by using tactics that <u>seem unfair</u>, but <u>aren't</u> against the rules.

<u>Gamesmanship</u> is <u>not</u> actually cheating — but it can come <u>quite close</u>. A lot of the techniques are about <u>breaking</u> up the <u>flow</u> of a game, or <u>distracting</u> your opponents:

1) <u>Time-wasting</u> in football is when players deliberately <u>faff about</u>. This <u>runs down</u> the <u>clock</u> and <u>breaks up</u> the <u>flow</u> of the game.

2) In tennis, some players make loud <u>grunting</u> or <u>shrieking</u> noises when they <u>hit the ball</u> to try and <u>intimidate</u> or <u>distract</u> their opponent.

3) In basketball, a manager might call a <u>timeout</u> just as the opposition win a <u>free throw</u>. This is to try and make them <u>overthink</u> the shot.

> <u>Deviance</u> is behaviour that goes against the <u>moral values</u> or <u>laws</u> of the sport.

<u>Deviance</u> is <u>breaking the rules</u>.
Sometimes it involves <u>cheating</u> to gain an <u>advantage</u> in the game:

1) Using <u>performance-enhancing drugs</u> (see the next page) is deviance because it gives you an <u>unfair</u> advantage.

2) '<u>Professional fouls</u>', like tripping someone to get ahead of them, are also deviance.

3) Other times it's being <u>violent</u> and <u>aggressive</u> — see the next page.

<u>Gamesmanship</u> does <u>not</u> normally result in <u>punishment</u> for the players, although if it is taken <u>too far</u> referees might get <u>involved</u>.

<u>Deviance</u> is <u>punished</u> by sports officials to <u>discourage</u> players from doing it:

1) For really <u>serious offences</u>, like using performance-enhancing drugs or biting, players may be <u>banned</u> from competing. There could also be a <u>hefty fine</u>.

2) For deviance like <u>fouling</u> an opponent, the referee or umpire may punish players by <u>removing</u> them from the field of play <u>temporarily</u> (e.g. by putting them in the '<u>sin bin</u>') or <u>permanently</u>.

Most forms of deviance happen <u>more</u> at the <u>higher levels</u> of a sport because there is so much <u>at stake</u> — e.g. the money and the fame brought about through the commercialisation of sport (see p37).

Footballers ought to be gracious in defeat — they use 'em enough...

I know, it's easy to get confused between sportsmanship and gamesmanship. Just remember that sportsmanship is about 'being a good sport'. Now, I've got an Exam Practice Question fresh from the oven and still warm for you.

Q1 Describe the difference between deviance and gamesmanship. [2 marks]

Ethical Issues in Sport

And now two of the more <u>unsavoury aspects</u> of sport to round off this section...

Performance-Enhancing Drugs can Improve Performance

1) Some performers use drugs to <u>improve</u> their performance and be more <u>successful</u> in their sport, which can lead to <u>wealth</u> and <u>fame</u>.

2) Some performers also claim they use drugs to <u>level the playing field</u> — if other competitors use drugs, you're at a disadvantage unless you use them too.

3) The use of these drugs in sport is usually <u>banned</u>, and they can have <u>nasty side effects</u>.

4) Unfortunately, some performers still <u>break the rules</u> by taking them anyway — even with the <u>risks</u> to their <u>health</u> and to their <u>reputation</u> if they're caught.

5) The use of performance-enhancing drugs can also harm the <u>reputation</u> and <u>credibility</u> of the <u>sport</u>.

6) These are the drugs you need to know about:

STIMULANTS

- Affect the <u>central nervous system</u> (the bits of your brain and spine that control your <u>reactions</u>).
- They can <u>increase mental</u> and <u>physical alertness</u>, and also <u>mask fatigue</u>.

But...

- They can lead to <u>high blood pressure</u>, <u>heart</u> and <u>liver problems</u>, and <u>strokes</u>.
- They're <u>addictive</u>.

<u>Cyclists</u> and <u>runners</u> might think that stimulants will help their performance.

ANABOLIC STEROIDS (AGENTS)

- Mimic the male sex hormone <u>testosterone</u>.
- Testosterone <u>increases</u> your <u>bone</u> and <u>muscle growth</u> (so you can get bigger and stronger). It can also make you more <u>aggressive</u>.

But...

- They can cause <u>high blood pressure</u>, <u>heart disease</u> and <u>infertility</u>, and can increase the risk of developing <u>cancer</u>.
- Women may grow <u>facial</u> and <u>body hair</u>, and their voice may <u>deepen</u>.

Anabolic steroids could be used by a <u>weightlifter</u> to gain an unfair advantage.

BETA BLOCKERS

- <u>Reduce heart rate</u>, <u>muscle tension</u>, <u>blood pressure</u> and the <u>effect of adrenaline</u>. This <u>steadies shaking hands</u>, which improves <u>fine motor skills</u>, and has a <u>calming</u>, <u>relaxing</u> effect.

But...

- They can cause <u>nausea</u>, <u>weakness</u>, <u>low blood pressure</u>, <u>cramp</u> and <u>heart failure</u>.
- They're <u>banned</u> in some sports and if allowed must be <u>prescribed</u> by a <u>medical professional</u>.

Athletes in sports requiring <u>accuracy</u>, e.g. shooting, golf and diving, might use beta blockers.

Player Violence is Bad... Obviously

<u>Violence</u> in sport can happen because players are <u>frustrated</u> with a result or with a <u>referee's decision</u>. It can also come from players being overly <u>emotional</u> or <u>competitive</u>, or as a response to, e.g. a <u>bad tackle</u>.

- Cuban taekwondo athlete Angel Matos was <u>banned</u> from the sport for life after deliberately <u>kicking a referee</u>.
- Boxer Mike Tyson and footballer Luis Suarez have both been in trouble for <u>biting</u> their opposition.

This drug is anabolic, it's diabolic — why it's health blighting...

Make sure you can give examples of performers in different sports who might use the drugs mentioned above.

Q1   Identify one performance-enhancing drug that an archer might use. Explain your choice.   [2 marks]

Revision Questions for Section Four

That's <u>Section Four</u> done and dusted — now be a <u>good sport</u> and have a go at these <u>revision questions</u>.

- Try these questions and <u>tick off each one</u> when you <u>get it right</u>.
- When you've done <u>all the questions</u> for a topic and are <u>completely happy</u> with it, tick off the topic.
- The answers can all be found by <u>looking back over pages 33 to 40</u>.

<u>Influences on Participation (p33-36)</u> ☑

1) Give an example of how the media can influence participation in sport. ☐
2) How can your gender influence what sports you participate in? ☐
3) Give one example of why a person's ethnicity or religion might affect their participation in sport. ☐
4) Outline one way that the amount of money you have could affect your participation in sport. ☐
5) Give one way that your family might influence your participation in sport. ☐
6) Describe two ways that your age can limit your participation in physical activities. ☐
7) Explain how someone's experience at school may affect whether they participate in sport as an adult. ☐
8) Give two ways that the environment you live in can affect what sports you take part in. ☐
9) Explain how sports participation rates can be improved by promotion, provision and access. ☐
10) How can the media help improve participation rates amongst the disabled? ☐
11) How do you spot an increase in a participation rate on a line graph? ☐

<u>Commercialisation of Sport (p37-38)</u> ☑

12) What does 'commercialisation' mean? ☐
13) Give one effect of increased media coverage on a sport. ☐
14) Give one advantage and one disadvantage of sponsorship for a sport. ☐
15) If a sports team gets media coverage, what might happen to the value of their sponsorship deals? Give a possible reason for this happening. ☐
16) How can increased media coverage increase participation in a sport? ☐
17) Why do companies sponsor sports? ☐
18) Give one way an athlete could lose their sponsorship deal. ☐
19) Which of these cannot sponsor a UK football team: a) a car manufacturer, b) a tobacco company? ☐
20) Give an advantage and a disadvantage of a brewery sponsoring a youth games tournament. ☐

<u>Ethical Issues in Sport (p39-40)</u> ☑

21) Give a definition and an example of:
   a) sportsmanship
   b) gamesmanship
   c) deviance ☐
22) Is time-wasting in football an example of gamesmanship or deviance? What about a 'professional foul'? ☐
23) Is deviance more likely or less likely to happen in the higher levels of sport? Why? ☐
24) Why would an athlete take each of these performance-enhancing drugs?
   a) anabolic steroids
   b) beta blockers
   c) stimulants ☐
25) Give two reasons why a player might be violent towards an opponent. ☐

Learning Skills

Learning movement skills and performing them well is really important in PE. This page is all about the different types of skill — buckle up, it's going to be a wild ride full of plenty of thrilling definitions...

A Motor Skill is Something You Learn that Involves Movement

1) Learn this definition:

> A MOTOR SKILL is a learned ability to use movement to bring about the result you want.

2) There are some characteristics that make a movement or performance skilful:

EFFICIENCY — A skilled movement should be efficient and use the minimum amount of energy/time. E.g. a good swimming technique can help you swim faster and for longer.

I meant to do that

PRE-DETERMINED — With any skilled movement, you always have a pre-determined result in mind — you know what you want to do before you start. E.g. if you're passing the ball in hockey you know what type of pass you're going to use and who you want to pass it to.

COORDINATED — Skilled movements are coordinated — they use two or more parts of the body together to get the maximum effect. E.g. a vault in gymnastics requires good arm and leg coordination to produce the necessary lift.

Man I'm gorgeous...

FLUENT — A skilled athlete is able to flow confidently from one skilled movement to another, e.g. punch combinations in boxing.

AESTHETIC — Skilled movements are controlled and look good. In some sports, like gymnastics and figure skating, your skill is judged by the appearance of your movements. Skilled players make skilled movements and techniques look easy, while less skilled players and performers can look awkward and uncoordinated.

Skills can be Classified in Different Ways

There are other ways of classifying skills, but you only need to know about these two.

1) Skills can be classified as open or closed, and as simple or complex.
2) Most skills come somewhere in between these classifications. You can show this by putting skills on a 'continuum' (or 'scale') with one category at each end.

OPEN VS CLOSED SKILLS — ENVIRONMENTAL CONTINUUM

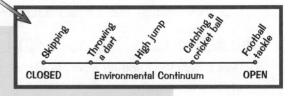

1) An open skill is performed in a changing environment, where a performer has to react and adapt to external factors. E.g. during a football tackle, you need to adapt to things such as the positions of other players on the pitch.
2) A closed skill is always performed in the same predictable environment — it's not affected by external factors. E.g. when breaking off in snooker, the conditions are the same every time.

SIMPLE VS COMPLEX SKILLS — DIFFICULTY CONTINUUM

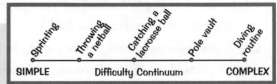

1) A simple skill is one which doesn't need much concentration or much information processing to do, e.g. running.
2) A complex skill is one which needs lots of concentration or lots of information processing to do, e.g. a volley in football.

Quick — get learning while there's skill time...

Phew — who knew there was so much to know about being skilful in sport... Have a go at this Practice Question.

Q1   Explain the importance of efficient technique for the skill of marathon running.   [2 marks]

Goal Setting

Setting <u>goals</u> and <u>targets</u> can often seem a bit of a hassle. But if you put the effort in and set them properly, not only do you have something to <u>aim</u> for, but reaching your targets can make you feel <u>ace</u>.

Goal Setting can Help you Train

<u>Goal setting</u> means setting <u>targets</u> that you want to reach. You might have a <u>long-term goal</u> and set yourself a series of <u>short-term goals</u> or targets to meet while <u>working</u> towards it.

There are a few reasons to set goals:

1) Setting goals helps you <u>stick</u> to your training <u>programme</u>.
2) Goal setting helps training by giving you something to <u>aim</u> for, which <u>motivates</u> you to work hard and keeps you <u>enthusiastic</u>.
3) Setting goals helps to <u>improve performance</u>.

Goal Setting Should be SMART

When you're setting targets make sure they're <u>SMART</u>.

S ➡ <u>SPECIFIC</u>: Say <u>exactly</u> what you want to achieve.
　1) You need to have a <u>specific</u> target and outline <u>exactly</u> what you need to do to achieve it.
　2) This makes sure you're <u>focused</u> on your goal.
　3) E.g. 'My goal is to swim 1000 m continuously'.

M ➡ <u>MEASURABLE</u>: Goals need to be <u>measurable</u>.
　1) This is so you can see <u>how much</u> you've progressed towards your goal over time — so you <u>stay motivated</u> to train.
　2) E.g. 'My goal is to run 100 m in under 12 seconds'.

A ➡ <u>ACHIEVABLE</u>: You need to make sure your targets are set at the right level of <u>difficulty</u>. If a target's <u>too difficult</u>, you might start to feel <u>negative</u> about your performance, and <u>give up</u>. However, if it is <u>too easy</u>, it won't <u>motivate</u> you.

R ➡ <u>RECORDED</u>: Set targets you can easily <u>keep track of</u>.
　1) Do this by making sure you keep a <u>log</u> of your aims and your progress.
　2) <u>Writing</u> down your <u>target</u> will make you less likely to be <u>distracted</u> from it.
　3) Also, being able to <u>track</u> your progress and see it <u>written down</u> will help to <u>motivate</u> you, meaning you have a greater chance of <u>reaching</u> your goal.

T ➡ <u>TIMED</u>: Set a <u>deadline</u> for reaching your goal.
　1) You need a time limit to make sure your target is <u>measurable</u>.
　2) Meeting <u>short-term</u> target deadlines keeps you on course to reach <u>long-term goals</u> in time.
　3) This keeps you <u>motivated</u> — you'll want to train to achieve your goal in time for a deadline.

As well as <u>setting targets</u>, you need to make sure you <u>review them</u> regularly. This is so you can see how much you've <u>progressed</u> towards your goal and <u>what else</u> you need to do to achieve it.

Goal setting — jumpers for goal posts...

Make sure you know what SMART stands for and how it can improve performance. Now try a Practice Question...

Q1 An athlete sets herself a goal to increase her running speed in six weeks.
State **one** principle of SMART goal setting that this goal does not apply. Explain your answer. [2 marks]

Goal Setting and Mental Preparation

Setting goals to aim for is pretty pointless if you don't <u>monitor</u> your <u>progress</u>. It's not all about the body though — <u>performing well</u> in sport is as much about <u>the mind</u>...

Data can be used to help Monitor your Progress

<u>Data</u> about your <u>performances</u> in <u>training</u> can help you to see whether or not you're <u>on track</u> to <u>meet your goals</u>. This is one of the reasons your <u>targets</u> need to be <u>measurable</u>. For example:

Nadège has just started cycling and she wants to <u>improve</u> her <u>average speed</u>. She sets herself a goal to increase her average speed by <u>4 km/h</u> in <u>12 weeks</u>.

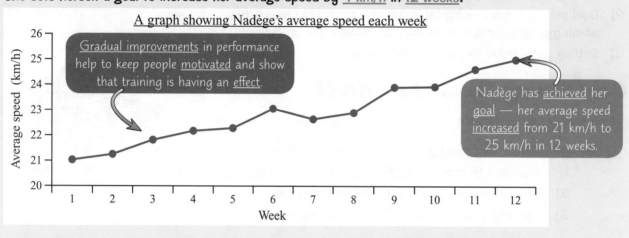

A graph showing Nadège's average speed each week

<u>Gradual improvements</u> in performance help to keep people <u>motivated</u> and show that training is having an <u>effect</u>.

Nadège has <u>achieved</u> her <u>goal</u> — her average speed <u>increased</u> from 21 km/h to 25 km/h in 12 weeks.

Having a <u>goal</u> to aim for helps <u>motivate</u> people to <u>keep training</u>. In turn, this means that they are far more <u>likely</u> to <u>achieve</u> their goal — because they are <u>sticking</u> to their <u>training</u> regime. It's a <u>win-win</u>...

You can Mentally Prepare for Sport

Now remember Lenny, stay focused on the game.

1) Being <u>mentally prepared</u> is all about being able to get in the 'zone'.

2) It can help you stay <u>focused</u>, <u>confident</u> and <u>motivated</u>, keep control of your emotions and <u>cope with stress</u> so you can perform at your best.

3) There are lots of different techniques to help you <u>mentally prepare</u>:

<u>IMAGERY</u> is used when you <u>imagine</u> doing something that <u>relaxes</u> you, or imagine <u>success</u> in order to increase confidence. It can improve <u>concentration</u> by blocking out <u>distractions</u>.
E.g. A football player <u>imagining</u> lifting the <u>trophy</u> after winning the final of a competition.

<u>SELECTIVE ATTENTION</u> is focusing on important things that will help you perform well, and <u>ignoring</u> things that <u>aren't important</u>.
E.g. A rugby player <u>blocking out</u> the noise of the <u>crowd</u> whilst kicking a conversion.

<u>POSITIVE THINKING</u> is telling yourself <u>positive things</u> that will <u>motivate</u> you or <u>reassure</u> you that you can <u>perform well</u>.
E.g. A marathon runner <u>thinking</u> about all the <u>training</u> they have done to <u>prepare</u> for a race.

<u>MENTAL REHEARSAL</u> is <u>imagining</u> the <u>feeling</u> in the <u>muscles</u> when <u>perfectly</u> performing a skill, or mentally <u>rehearsing</u> the <u>skills</u> needed. It can <u>prepare</u> you to react or perform.
E.g. A diver going over the <u>sequence</u> of <u>movements</u> for their dive in their head.

4) Practising your skills during a <u>warm-up</u> can also help you mentally prepare (see page 30).

Mentally rehearse your exam for guaranteed success...

Being mentally prepared can really help your performance — so it's lucky that there are some handy techniques to help you on your way to being mentally ready for sport. Learn all about them, then try this Practice Question.

Q1 Suggest **two** ways that a football player might use mental rehearsal before taking a penalty. [2 marks]

Types of Guidance

To learn or improve a skill, you might need some guidance to help you.

Performers *Need Guidance* to Develop *Skills*

There are lots of different types of guidance a coach or trainer can give:

Have a look at p42 for definitions of the different skill types.

1) <u>VISUAL</u> — <u>Visual clues</u> to help you perform a technique.

ADVANTAGES

1) Works well for <u>beginners</u> — they can <u>copy</u> the skill.
2) Can be used to teach skills that can be broken down — each part of the skill can be shown <u>step by step</u>.

E.g. A coach could use <u>demonstrations</u> or <u>videos</u> and <u>diagrams</u> to show how a technique should be performed.

DISADVANTAGES

1) Less useful for teaching <u>complex</u> skills — they're harder <u>to copy</u>.
2) Difficult to show skills that can't be <u>broken down</u>.

2) <u>VERBAL</u> — An explanation in <u>words</u> of how to perform a technique.

ADVANTAGES

1) Can be <u>combined</u> with other types of guidance.
2) Helpful for <u>experienced performers</u> who'll understand any technical language.
3) Can give guidance <u>during</u> a performance. This is especially useful for improving <u>open skills</u>.

E.g. A coach could <u>communicate</u> to players from the sideline during netball practice.

DISADVANTAGES

1) Less useful for teaching <u>complex</u> skills which are difficult to explain.
2) Could be <u>confusing</u> for a beginner if it uses <u>complicated language</u>.

Pass the ball!

3) <u>MANUAL</u> — When the coach <u>physically moves</u> your body <u>through</u> the <u>technique</u>.

ADVANTAGES

1) You can get the "<u>feel</u>" of a skill before doing it on your own.
2) Works well to teach people of <u>all skill levels</u>.

Learning by doing an action is known as kinaesthetic learning.

DISADVANTAGES

1) A performer could start to <u>rely</u> on it and not be able to perform a skill <u>without</u> it.
2) Difficult to use in <u>large groups</u>.

E.g. A coach might <u>guide</u> your arms when you're <u>practising</u> a golf swing, or the shot put.

4) <u>MECHANICAL</u> — Guidance given using <u>sport equipment</u>.

ADVANTAGES

1) Useful for teaching <u>beginners</u> — they can feel <u>safe</u> while practising a new skill that might normally be <u>dangerous</u>.
2) Helpful for teaching <u>complex</u> skills.

DISADVANTAGES

1) A learner might be <u>unable</u> to perform the skill without the help of the <u>equipment</u>.
2) Difficult to use in <u>large groups</u>.

E.g. You might use a <u>harness</u> in trampolining to practise a somersault for the first time.

Verbal guidance is just what it sounds like...

Make sure you know the advantages and disadvantages of these guidance types. In the exam you might need to be able to give practical examples of each type too. Here's an Exam Practice Question to try...

Q1* Evaluate the use of verbal and manual guidance to improve a beginner's performance in golf.   [6 marks]

Types of Feedback

Another way to improve a skill is to get feedback. Feedback can be used to work out your strengths and weaknesses and to come up with an action plan to improve your performance.

Feedback — Finding Out How You Did

Feedback is information that is given to a performer about their performance. It can help to improve future performances. There are several different types of feedback:

Feedback can Come From Different Places

Feedback could come from your own judgement, or from someone who was watching you perform.

INTRINSIC FEEDBACK — you know how well you did the technique because of what it 'felt' like. This works best for experienced performers — they can judge whether or not they've performed well.

EXTRINSIC FEEDBACK — someone else tells you or shows you what happened, and how to improve. This is suited to beginners — they don't have the experience or knowledge to accurately assess their own performance.

E.g. A gymnast may feel that they are off-balance whilst doing a beam routine.

E.g. A football player can hear feedback from the coach, who is on the sideline.

Feedback can Focus on Different Aspects of a Skill

The information in feedback can focus on different parts of a skill or movement. It might focus on:

KNOWLEDGE OF PERFORMANCE — did you use the correct movements/technique? This can be extrinsic or intrinsic. This type of feedback works well for experienced performers — it helps them to 'fine-tune' a skill that they can already perform.

KNOWLEDGE OF RESULTS — what was the outcome? This is always extrinsic and can include data, e.g. your time in a race. This is useful for inexperienced performers — they need to be told whether or not they achieved the right result.

E.g. A diver may feel that their routine went smoothly as each move went well.

E.g. A long jumper is told the distance they travelled.

Feedback can Focus on Positives or Negatives

Feedback can focus on the good parts of a skill or movement, or the bad parts.

POSITIVE FEEDBACK — focuses on what you did well. This is better for beginners — it helps them remember which parts of the movement they should repeat.

NEGATIVE FEEDBACK — focuses on what you didn't do well and could improve. It can be useful for experienced performers — it provides them with information that they can use to fine-tune their performance and on which to base goals. It's better to avoid too much negative feedback with beginners as it can put them off learning the skill.

E.g. A coach may tell a beginner that they have a good technique.

E.g. A coach may give feedback about the errors in a trampolining routine.

I'd make a PE joke — but it would only get negative feedback...

Make sure you learn which types of feedback work best for different skill levels. Here's a Practice Question to try.

Q1   A snowboarding instructor praises a beginner's stance on the snowboard. Identify the type of feedback this is and justify its use in helping the beginner learn to snowboard.   [3 marks]

Revision Questions for Section Five

Section Five has come to an end, so let's see how much you've learned.

- Try these questions and tick off each one when you get it right.
- When you've done all the questions for a topic and are completely happy with it, tick off the topic.
- The answers can all be found by looking back over pages 42-46.

Learning Skills (p42) ☑

1) Pre-determined is a characteristic of a skilful movement. What is meant by this? ☑
2) What is the difference between an open and a closed skill? ☑
3) Give an example of an open skill and an example of a closed skill. ☑
4) Which type of skill needs lots of concentration to perform? ☑

Goal Setting and Mental Preparation (p43-44) ☑

5) Why might a performer set themselves a goal? ☑
6) What do the letters in SMART stand for? ☑
7) Explain the meaning and benefits of each element of SMART. ☑
8) Why should you review your targets and goals regularly? ☑
9) Give four techniques that an athlete might use to mentally prepare for a performance. ☑

Types of Guidance (p45) ☑

10) What is guidance? ☑
11) What is visual guidance? Why is it not suited to complex skills? ☑
12) What is verbal guidance and why is it more suited to more experienced performers? ☑
13) Give an example of manual guidance. ☑
14) What is mechanical guidance? ☑
15) Give a disadvantage that manual and mechanical guidance have in common. ☑

Types of Feedback (p46) ☑

16) What is feedback? ☑
17) Explain what is meant by:
   a) Intrinsic feedback
   b) Extrinsic feedback ☑
18) What is the difference between knowledge of performance and knowledge of results? ☑
19) Why is negative feedback not suited for use with beginners? ☑
20) Is knowledge of results an example of intrinsic or extrinsic feedback? Explain why. ☑

Health, Fitness and Well-Being

Regular physical activity helps you to be <u>healthy</u> by improving your <u>physical</u>, <u>emotional</u> and <u>social</u> health and well-being. First up, what health and well-being are...

Fitness is just One Part of being Healthy

1) Being healthy is <u>more</u> than just having a healthy body — if you're always unhappy, then you're not healthy. Don't take my word for it though — here's the definition used by the <u>World Health Organisation</u> (WHO):

> <u>Health</u> is a state of complete <u>physical</u>, <u>mental</u> and <u>social well-being</u> and <u>not</u> merely the absence of disease or infirmity.

> The term 'emotional well-being' is often used instead of 'mental well-being'.

> There's more on emotional and social health and well-being on the next page.

2) <u>Well-being</u> can be a tricky concept to define, but one way is:

> <u>Well-being</u> is the state of feeling <u>content</u>, <u>happy</u> and <u>healthy</u>.

3) So if you have a good level of <u>well-being</u>, you feel <u>positive</u> and <u>satisfied</u> with life.

4) <u>Fitness</u> is one part of <u>good health</u> — here's the definition:

> <u>Fitness</u> is the ability to meet the <u>demands of the environment</u>.

So, being fit means you're <u>physically able</u> to do whatever you <u>want</u> or <u>need</u> to do, without getting tired quickly.

5) Fitness <u>helps</u> with <u>physical</u> health, but you can have a <u>high</u> level of fitness <u>without</u> necessarily being physically healthy — e.g. some athletes <u>overtrain</u> and end up getting <u>injured</u>.

There are Many Physical Benefits of Exercise

<u>Regular physical activity</u> has a wide range of <u>physical</u> benefits:

1) Regular <u>aerobic</u> exercise helps prevent <u>high blood pressure</u> (<u>hypertension</u>) by keeping your <u>heart</u> strong and <u>arteries</u> elastic, and helping to <u>remove cholesterol</u> from artery walls.

2) This means <u>blood</u> can <u>flow easily</u> round the body, which <u>reduces</u> the risk of <u>coronary heart disease (CHD)</u>.

As you get older, your bone density <u>decreases</u>, which increases the likelihood of bone <u>fractures</u>. <u>Weight-bearing</u> exercise, where your <u>legs</u> and <u>feet</u> support your whole body weight (like aerobics or running), helps to <u>strengthen</u> your bones by increasing <u>bone density</u>.

Regular exercise helps prevent <u>obesity</u>, by using up <u>energy</u> that your body would otherwise store as <u>fat</u> (see p51).

<u>Type-2 diabetes</u> is a disease that gives you a <u>high blood sugar level</u>, and your risk of developing it <u>increases</u> drastically as you get <u>older</u>. Your blood sugar level is <u>controlled</u> by a hormone called <u>insulin</u>. If you have diabetes, this means you don't have <u>enough</u> insulin or your body's cells <u>aren't reacting</u> to insulin properly (they're <u>insulin-resistant</u>).

Regular exercise helps you <u>avoid</u> diabetes in <u>two</u> ways, by:

1) Helping you maintain a <u>healthy weight</u>. This makes you far <u>less likely</u> to get diabetes.

2) <u>Increasing</u> your cells' <u>sensitivity</u> to insulin, which <u>reduces</u> the chance of becoming <u>insulin-resistant</u>.

Exercise benefits your <u>musculo-skeletal system</u> — <u>muscles</u> and <u>bones</u> get stronger, and <u>joints</u> more flexible. This makes <u>injury</u> less likely and improves your <u>posture</u>.

Exercise improves your <u>components of fitness</u> (p19-21), so you can exercise more <u>intensely</u> and for <u>longer</u>.

All these benefits of exercise and I'm sitting around writing jokes...

Now you know the physical benefits of exercise, get in a quick brain workout with this Exam Practice Question...

Q1   Explain **one** way that regular exercise helps to prevent type-2 diabetes.   [2 marks]

Health, Fitness and Well-Being

As well as making you into a Schwarzenegger-like picture of physical health, exercise is great for your emotional and social health. You need to be able to give examples of how it helps.

Emotional Health is about how you Feel

1) Being healthy is more than just having a body that works well — you also have to take into account how you feel. Your emotional health and well-being is based on how you feel about yourself and how you respond to different situations.

2) Taking part in physical activity and sport can have emotional benefits:

SELF-ESTEEM AND CONFIDENCE

1) Physical activity can increase your self-esteem (your opinion of yourself) and confidence and generally make you feel better about yourself, e.g. if you feel you've achieved something.

2) It also releases 'feel good' hormones, which can make you feel happier about yourself.

IMAGE

Seeing improvements in your physical health, e.g. losing weight or gaining strength, can improve your self-image.

STRESS MANAGEMENT

Doing physical activity can help relieve stress and tension by taking your mind off whatever's worrying you and by making you feel happier. This helps prevent stress-related illnesses. This could be especially helpful for younger people, whose schoolwork or jobs are a source of stress.

> Improvements in self-esteem and self-image can be particularly beneficial for older people, who might be struggling to accept how their bodies have changed over time.

Dave herds cats for a living, so he does one bicep-curl every time he's stressed...

Social Health is about how you Relate to Society

1) Your social health and well-being is about how you interact with others and form relationships.

2) There can be plenty of social benefits from doing physical activity and sport:

FRIENDSHIP

Doing physical activity can help you make friends with people of different ages and backgrounds. For example, some elderly folk may have limited opportunities to socialise, so sport can be a great way to make new friends. It's also a great way of socialising with your current friends.

COMBATTING LONELINESS

Elderly people are particularly at risk of becoming lonely, so building bonds through exercise and sport can be very helpful for them.

BELONGING TO A GROUP

Taking part in team activities like football, can increase your sense of belonging. Sharing a common interest and working together can increase the social bonds between team members and can also help you to feel more involved in society as a whole. Young children can really benefit from team sports as they need to learn how to interact and work with others.

> So you kick them in the shin and I'll steal the ball...

I joined an aerobic tidying class — it's a real mess reliever...

These benefits are less obvious than those on the last page — especially the social health ones. But take your time and jot them down again and again until you've got them all stored in your head. Then try this Practice Question...

Q1 Give **two** emotional health benefits of exercise.

[2 marks]

Sedentary Lifestyles

Couch potatoes be warned — sitting still all day <u>isn't</u> good for you. Apart from sitting still all day <u>revising</u> that is...

A Sedentary Lifestyle has Many Long-Term Health Risks

If you have a <u>sedentary lifestyle</u>, it means you don't exercise <u>enough</u>:

A <u>SEDENTARY LIFESTYLE</u> is one where there is <u>irregular</u> or <u>no physical activity</u>.

It's important that you try to <u>avoid</u> living a <u>sedentary</u> lifestyle, as the <u>consequences</u> can be <u>serious</u>.

- Emotional health problems like <u>low confidence</u>, <u>poor body image</u> and <u>depression</u>.
- Accelerated <u>bone density loss</u> which increases the chances of <u>injuries</u> like fractures.
- Poor <u>posture</u> which can cause <u>back</u>, <u>neck</u> and <u>shoulder</u> pain.
- Poor <u>social</u> health — it becomes <u>hard</u> to leave the home and <u>socialise</u> with others.
- <u>Obesity</u> (having a large amount of body fat), which can lead to many <u>other</u> physical health problems.

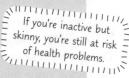

1) <u>Obesity</u> puts <u>strain</u> on your <u>cardiovascular</u> system and decreases <u>cardiovascular endurance</u>.
2) Increased body fat can lead to <u>high cholesterol</u> and <u>fatty deposits</u> in the <u>arteries</u>, making it <u>harder</u> for the heart to pump blood. This can lead to <u>hypertension</u> (high blood pressure) and <u>coronary heart disease</u>.
3) You are more likely to develop <u>type-2 diabetes</u> if you are obese (see p48).
4) Being overweight <u>decreases flexibility</u>, <u>speed</u>, <u>power</u> and <u>agility</u>, so affects your <u>performance</u> too.

If you're inactive but skinny, you're still at risk of health problems.

Data About Health Issues can be Plotted on a Graph

You can <u>analyse</u> data on health issues to understand how things are <u>changing over time</u>. This allows you to spot <u>trends</u> and make predictions about the <u>future</u>.

Here's an example of the kind of graph you could get in your <u>exam</u>:

This trend is out of control...

- You can either <u>describe</u> what's happening <u>over time</u> (see <u>1</u>), or at certain <u>points in time</u> (see <u>2</u> and <u>3</u>).
- Be <u>specific</u> — give the <u>exact</u> dates for the part of the graph you're describing — e.g. 'in 2010', 'from 1993 to 2009'.
- Make sure you say <u>enough</u> to get <u>all</u> the <u>marks</u>.
- If you're asked to <u>describe</u> a <u>trend</u> from a graph, you need to look at the graph <u>as a whole</u> to see whether it is <u>going up</u> or <u>going down</u> overall. You may also need to <u>predict</u> whether the trend is likely to <u>continue</u>. E.g. in the graph above, there's a general <u>upward trend</u> in obesity rates for men and women. This trend looks like it will <u>continue</u>.

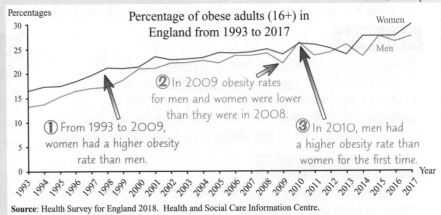

Source: Health Survey for England 2018. Health and Social Care Information Centre.

Sedentary? Not me — I get up and put the kettle on sometimes...

It is important to avoid a sedentary lifestyle by staying active. Make sure you learn all the health risks on this page, then hop to it and try this Exam Practice Question...

Q1 State **two** long-term health risks that are increased by a sedentary lifestyle.   [2 marks]

Diet and Nutrition

To stay healthy you need a balanced diet — this means getting the right amount of nutrients for your lifestyle.

You Should Eat a Balanced Diet to be Healthy

1) Eating a balanced diet is an important part of being healthy and helps you perform well in sport.

2) What makes up a balanced diet is slightly different for everyone, depending on how active you are.

> A balanced diet contains the best ratio of nutrients to match your lifestyle.

3) The 'best ratio' means the right amount of each nutrient in relation to the other nutrients. There isn't one type of 'superfood' that has everything your body needs — you need a mix of foods.

4) A balanced diet supports your lifestyle by providing the nutrients your body needs for energy, growth and hydration. It helps prevent health problems and injury, and to speed up recovery following exercise.

5) Your body needs large amounts of carbohydrates, fats and proteins. The pie chart below shows the rough proportions of each that an average person should eat as part of a balanced diet:

FATS

1) Fats are made from molecules called fatty acids.

2) They provide more energy than carbohydrates for low-intensity exercise. They also help to keep the body warm and protect organs, which helps to prevent injury.

3) Some vitamins can only be absorbed by the body using fats.

4) Too many saturated fats can cause obesity.

Proteins (15-20%)
Fats (25-30%)
Carbohydrates (55-60%)

Oh, I'm very complex y'know.

CARBOHYDRATES

1) For most people, carbohydrates are the main source of energy for the body. Carbohydrates are vital for providing energy for your muscles during physical activity.

2) You can get simple ones like sugar, and complex ones, e.g. starch, from bread, pasta or rice. Complex carbohydrates release energy steadily over longer periods than simple carbohydrates.

3) Whenever you eat carbohydrates, some will get used by the body straight away.

4) The rest gets stored in the liver and muscles as a compound called glycogen, ready for when it's needed (or turned into fat).

PROTEINS

1) Proteins help the body grow and repair itself. They're vital for building and repairing muscles after exercise.

2) They're made from molecules called amino acids — your body can make new proteins from the amino acids in food.

3) Meat, fish, eggs and beans are all rich in protein.

A balanced diet — dead important for tight-rope walkers...

Make sure that you understand how carbohydrates, proteins and fats help you to do physical activity.

Q1 State **one** reason why carbohydrates are needed by the body. [1 mark]

Diet and Nutrition

It's all well and good making sure that you are getting your fill of <u>fats</u>, <u>carbohydrates</u> and <u>proteins</u>, but you won't last long without the stuff on this page.

You need Small Amounts of Vitamins and Minerals

VITAMINS

1) Vitamins help your bones, teeth, skin and other tissues to <u>grow</u>. They're also needed for many of the body's <u>chemical reactions</u>, e.g. some are used in the processes that release energy from food.

2) <u>Fat-soluble</u> vitamins can be stored in the body. Here are a couple of examples:
   - <u>Vitamin A</u> — needed for your <u>growth</u> and <u>vision</u>.
   - <u>Vitamin D</u> — needed for <u>strong bones</u>, so helps to prevent <u>injury</u>.

3) <u>Water-soluble</u> vitamins can't be stored, so you need to eat them regularly. For example:
   - <u>Vitamin C</u> — good for your <u>skin</u> and helps to hold your <u>body tissues</u> together. It's also really important for your <u>immune system</u>, so helps you to <u>stay healthy</u> so you can train and perform well.

Earl   Mini-earl

MINERALS

1) Needed for healthy <u>bones</u> and <u>teeth</u>, and to build other <u>tissues</u>.

2) Minerals help in various <u>chemical reactions</u> in the body:
   - <u>Calcium</u> — needed for strong <u>bones</u> and <u>teeth</u>, and also for <u>muscle contraction</u>.
   - <u>Iron</u> — used in making <u>red blood cells</u>, which carry oxygen round the body, e.g. to the muscles.

Water is Really Important

WATER

1) Water is needed in loads of <u>chemical reactions</u> in the body. It's also used in sweat to help you <u>cool down</u> when your body temperature rises, e.g. through exercise. As well as <u>sweating</u>, you also lose water through your <u>breath</u>, <u>urine</u> and <u>faeces</u>.

2) If you don't drink enough to replace the water you've <u>used</u> or <u>lost</u>, you become <u>dehydrated</u>. This means your body <u>doesn't</u> have <u>enough water</u> to work well — it's not <u>hydrated</u>. This can cause:
   - <u>Blood thickening</u> — you guessed it, the blood gets thicker (more viscous). This makes it <u>harder</u> for the <u>heart</u> to pump the blood around — it has to work harder and beat faster. It also decreases the flow of <u>oxygen</u> to the muscles, so you can't perform as well.
   - An <u>increase</u> in <u>body temperature</u>, as without enough water the body can't sweat effectively. This can cause <u>overheating</u> and maybe even <u>fainting</u> through <u>heat exhaustion</u>.
   - <u>Muscle fatigue</u> and <u>cramps</u>, which could mean you have to stop doing an activity.
   - <u>Slower reactions</u> and <u>poor decision-making</u>, as your <u>brain</u> needs water to function well.

3) <u>Rehydration</u> with water or sports drinks <u>during</u> and <u>after</u> physical activity helps avoid dehydration. This is important in <u>endurance events</u> and <u>hot climates</u> where you <u>sweat more</u>.

4) Sports drinks have <u>sugar</u> in them to <u>replace</u> the energy your muscles have used up. They also contain a bit of <u>salt</u> which helps the water rehydrate you quickly.

5) If you drink too much water, you can become <u>overhydrated</u>. This can lead to <u>headaches</u>, <u>nausea</u> and <u>confusion</u>.

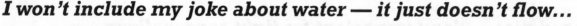

I won't include my joke about water — it just doesn't flow...

Make sure you understand the importance of water balance and the consequences of dehydration. Then time for a little Exam Practice Question? I think so...

Q1 Explain why hydration is important for a cross-country runner. [2 marks]

Diet and Nutrition

Next up is fibre, then there's all about how different <u>activities</u> need different amounts of <u>energy</u> and <u>nutrients</u>.

Don't Forget about Fibre

FIBRE

1) You need fibre to keep your <u>digestive system</u> working properly. Good digestion means that your body gets all the <u>nutrients</u> it needs from food, so you're healthy and can do physical activity.

2) There's lots of fibre in <u>fruit</u> and <u>vegetables</u> — another good reason to eat loads of them.

Intestine Express

Your Energy Intake and Usage Controls Your Weight

How much energy you need also depends on how much you use up through <u>bodily processes</u> (like breathing and digestion), <u>daily activities</u> and <u>exercise</u>. <u>Age</u> and <u>body size</u> affect this too.

- If you <u>don't</u> take in <u>enough</u> food to match the energy you need, your body <u>makes up the difference</u> by using up the energy stored in <u>body fat</u> and you <u>lose weight</u>.

- If you take in <u>more</u> energy than you <u>use</u>, the <u>spare</u> energy is stored as <u>fat</u>, which causes you to <u>gain weight</u>.

- If you want to <u>maintain</u> a healthy weight, you need to make sure the energy you take in <u>matches</u> the energy you use up.

Loving my new balanced diet!

Different Types of Physical Activity Require Different Nutrients

The type of <u>physical activity</u> you are doing affects the <u>balance of nutrients</u> you need.

ENDURANCE

If your activity involves long periods of <u>continuous exercise</u>, like competing in a triathlon, you need a diet rich in <u>carbohydrates</u>. This is because carbohydrates provide plenty of <u>energy</u> that is easily available for your muscles.

<u>Fat</u> is also an important <u>energy source</u> for <u>endurance athletes</u> as it can provide energy for <u>low</u> to <u>moderate intensity</u> exercise when supplies of carbohydrates are <u>running low</u>.

MUSCLE GROWTH

If your activity involves gaining <u>muscle bulk</u> — like <u>sprinting</u> or <u>weightlifting</u>, you need a diet rich in <u>protein</u> in order to <u>build</u> and <u>repair</u> your muscles.

DANGER Muscle Under Construction

1) Carrying around <u>extra</u> weight as <u>fat</u> can affect performance. So, for many physical activities, you will want a <u>diet</u> that helps keep body fat <u>low</u>.

2) <u>Hydration</u> (the body having the right amount of <u>water</u>) is really important when you're exercising (see p52). It's especially important to take in water during activities where you <u>sweat</u> a lot and have an increased <u>breathing rate</u> for a long period of <u>time</u>.

All this revision can be berry exhausting...

... but pear with it — you're doing grape! Reading the content over and over until you remember it is the kiwi to success. Now lettuce try this Exam Practice Question.

Q1   Justify whether a weightlifter or a triathlete would benefit more from a high carbohydrate diet.   [3 marks]

Revision Questions for Section Six

That's it for Section Six. Give yourself a little time to digest all that information (ho ho ho), then fingers on buzzers for the Section Six revision questions...

- Try these questions and tick off each one when you get it right.
- When you've done all the questions for a topic and are completely happy with it, tick off the topic.
- The answers can all be found by looking back over pages 48 to 53.

Health, Fitness and Well-Being (p48-49) ☑

1) Give two physical health benefits of physical activity. ☑
2) What effect does regular aerobic exercise have on blood pressure? ☑
3) Which type of exercise can help strengthen your bones? ☑
4) How can exercise make you feel good? ☑
5) Physical activity can increase your confidence. Is this a physical, emotional or social benefit? ☑
6) Give two social health benefits of sport. ☑

Sedentary Lifestyles (p50) ☑

7) Define a 'sedentary lifestyle'. ☑
8) Name an emotional health problem that is linked to a sedentary lifestyle. ☑
9) Explain why a sedentary lifestyle can lead to injury. ☑
10) Describe two physical health problems linked to obesity. ☑

Diet and Nutrition (p51-53) ☑

11) What is a 'balanced diet'? ☑
12) Explain why the perfect balanced diet isn't exactly the same for everyone. ☑
13) How does protein help you recover after exercise? ☐
14) Which nutrients provide your body with energy? ☑
15) True or false? Vitamins are needed in huge quantities. ☑
16) Give two negative effects of dehydration on sports performance. ☑
17) Explain what happens to your blood when you become dehydrated. ☑
18) State two effects of overhydration. ☑
19) What role does fibre play in a balanced diet? ☑
20) What type of athlete requires a diet that is high in carbohydrates? ☑
21) Why might a sprinter have a diet high in protein? ☑

Using Data

You've got to be comfortable with interpreting data displayed in graphs and tables. Luckily for you, these three pages will go through how you do it. And you thought you could get away from maths by taking PE...

There Are Two Different Types of Data

You can collect two different types of data — qualitative data and quantitative data:

The easiest way to remember the difference is 'quantitative' sounds like 'quantity' — which means 'number of'...

> Qualitative data describes something — it will be in words.

> Quantitative data measures something — it will be in numbers.

1) Qualitative data can be collected through observation — e.g. 'the team played well', 'the athlete is strong' or 'the weather was cold'.

2) Or you can interview people. E.g. asking an athlete how they're feeling before a race might give you answers like "confident" or "well-prepared".

3) It's less easy to analyse than data in numbers.

1) Quantitative data measures things — e.g. 'time taken to finish a race' or 'weight of an athlete'.

2) All the fitness tests (see pages 22-24) give quantitative data, as the results are numbers. You can also use surveys to collect quantitative data.

3) Quantitative data can be represented in tables and graphs, and analysed easily.

Analyse Graphs to spot Trends

Technicolour shorts are totally in right now...

Quantitative data is made up of numbers, so you can talk about increases and decreases, and highest and lowest values. This can also help you to spot trends and make predictions.

> A trend is when a graph is generally going up or down over time.

Here's an example of how data on performance can be analysed as part of feedback (see p46), to help a performer improve.

Predicting a trend can be tough.

1) To determine a trend, look at the data as a whole to spot the pattern.

2) Both lines are going up, so they show upward trends — the number of tackles made by both players is increasing over time.

For another example of analysing data over time see p36.

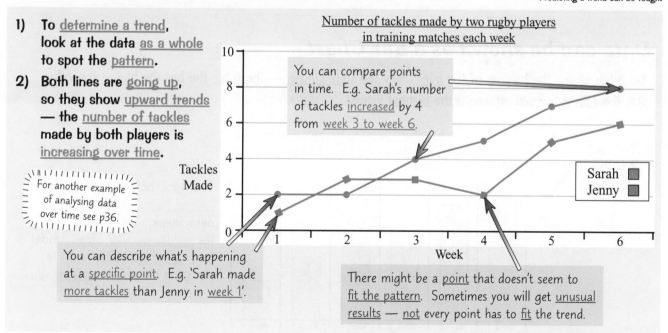

Number of tackles made by two rugby players in training matches each week

You can compare points in time. E.g. Sarah's number of tackles increased by 4 from week 3 to week 6.

Sarah
Jenny

You can describe what's happening at a specific point. E.g. 'Sarah made more tackles than Jenny in week 1'.

There might be a point that doesn't seem to fit the pattern. Sometimes you will get unusual results — not every point has to fit the trend.

Trends about data — amount of boredom is increasing over time...

Just from my experiences writing this page, I can promise you that it's frustratingly easy to mix up the words qualitative and quantitative, so double-check you're using the right one. Exam Practice Question time...

Q1 Using the line graph above, identify which person had the bigger increase in tackles made from week 2 to week 6.

[1 mark]

Using Data

Using data to help you plan and evaluate fitness training is dead important, so here's a whole page on it. You need to understand what the data is showing you, as well as using your knowledge about physical fitness.

You can Analyse your Fitness over Time

1) You can measure the effect of your training by doing regular fitness tests, and comparing the data you get over time.

2) You need to be able to describe what the data shows, and say what this means about the training — i.e. if it's working or what changes are needed.

3) Here's an example of the kind of thing you might see in the exam:

Bryan is doing a training programme to improve his cardiovascular fitness and his muscular endurance...

Bryan

Bryan's Fitness Test Results

Fitness Test	Weeks					
	1	2	3	4	5	6
Cooper 12-Minute Run (distance in m)	1450	1490	1530	1600	1640	1690
1-Minute Sit-up Test (no. of sit-ups)	45	46	45	46	44	45

The Cooper Run data shows that Bryan is doing better at the Cooper 12-minute Run Test each week — he is running further in 12 minutes. So the training is improving Bryan's cardiovascular fitness.

The sit-up data shows that the number of sit-ups Bryan can do is staying about the same, so the training is not improving his abdominal muscular endurance. This means Bryan may want to change his training programme to include more exercises that help improve his abdominal muscular endurance.

For more on fitness testing and training methods, see Section Three.

You can also look at national averages or ratings tables to understand how your scores in fitness tests compare with others in your age group or gender. For an example of this, see page 22.

Data can be shown as a Bar Chart

On a bar chart, the heights of the bars show the data values — the taller the bar the higher the value. So, the tallest bar will represent the highest value.

Week 1 has the tallest bar, so Bryan's resting heart rate was highest in week 1.

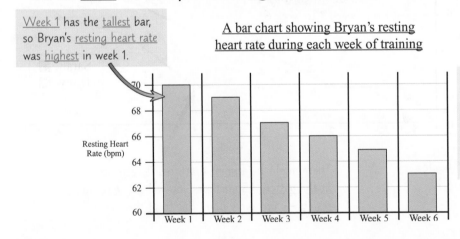

A bar chart showing Bryan's resting heart rate during each week of training

The trend here is that Bryan's resting heart rate is decreasing each week. This means that his cardiovascular fitness must be improving, as his heart is pumping blood more efficiently.

Top of the charts again — give it up for the 'tallest bars'...

It's really important you get good at using data about fitness to evaluate how effective an exercise programme is. Have another look over pages 22-24 to check you know all the fitness tests. Then do this Practice Question...

Q1 Using the bar chart above, what is Bryan's resting heart rate in week 4?

A 70 bpm   **B** 66 bpm   **C** 67 bpm   **D** 100 bpm   [1 mark]

Using Data

More data? Well okay, go on then — I know how much you love it. This page is about delicious pie charts and more ways to use data in training... Needless to say, you have to learn it all, tasty or not so tasty...

You can Look at Data for Large Groups of People

You can also use data to understand what's going on for large groups of people.

1) Pie charts are a good way to compare different categories.
2) The amount of the whole chart a section takes up tells you the percentage in that category — the whole chart represents 100% (everybody).
3) These charts show that the netball club is almost entirely female, the football club is mostly male, and the badminton club is 50% male and 50% female.

For examples of using data to understand trends on a large scale, see pages 36 and 50.

Percentage of members of three sports clubs who are male and female

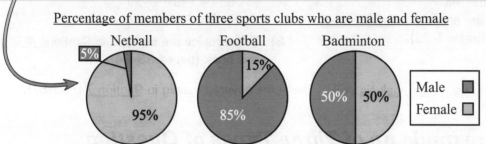

Remember, percentages tell you the proportion of people in a category, not the actual number.

Heart Rate Data can be used to work out Exercise Intensities

Analysing data about someone's heart rate during exercise can give you information about how intense their exercise is. It can also be used to see how quickly someone recovers from exercise. E.g.:

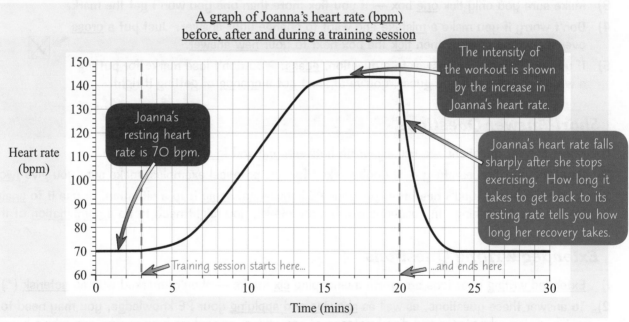

The intensity of the workout is shown by the increase in Joanna's heart rate.

Joanna's resting heart rate is 70 bpm.

Joanna's heart rate falls sharply after she stops exercising. How long it takes to get back to its resting rate tells you how long her recovery takes.

There is sometimes more than one person's heart rate displayed on the same graph.
This is handy as you can compare their fitness levels by looking at the difference in their resting heart rates.
You can also see how hard they worked during the session by the highest points that their heart rates reach.

Mmmmmm — pie charts...

That's it, the data section is over. I know, time flies when you're having fun. One last Practice Question for you...

Q1 Using the line graph above, state how long Joanna's heart rate was at least double her resting heart rate. Give your answer to the nearest minute. [1 mark]

Answering Exam Questions

Hurray — you made it to the end of the book. Now there's just the (ahem) exams left to go...

You'll Sit Two Exams for PE

1) Each paper tests you on one component of GCSE PE, lasts one hour and is worth 60 marks:

Paper 1 — Component 1	Paper 2 — Component 2
1) Component 1 is called 'Physical Factors Affecting Performance'.	1) Component 2 is called 'Socio-Cultural Issues and Sports Psychology'.
2) It includes the topics: • Applied anatomy and physiology • Physical training	2) It includes the topics: • Socio-cultural influences • Sports psychology • Health, fitness and well-being
3) These topics are covered in Sections 1-3 of this book (pages 1-32).	3) These topics are covered in Sections 4-6 of this book (pages 33-54).

2) Both papers will test your data analysis skills. These are covered mainly in Section 7 (p55-57).

Your Exams are made up of Three Types of Question

Multiple-Choice — Tick the Right Box

1) The multiple-choice questions give you a choice of four possible answers to the question. All you need to do is tick the box next to the correct answer. They're worth one mark each.

2) Sounds easy enough, but you still need to really know your stuff to be able to get them right.

3) Make sure you only tick one box — if you tick more than one you won't get the mark.

4) Don't worry if you make a mistake and want to change your answer. Just put a cross over the wrong answer, then tick the box next to your new answer.

5) If you don't know the answer to a question, guess. You don't lose marks for putting a wrong answer — if you guess, you've at least got a chance of getting it right.

Short-Answer Questions

1) Short-answer questions are usually worth between one and four marks.

2) Read the question carefully — if you're asked for two practical examples, make sure you give two.

3) To get the marks, you'll need to show your PE knowledge, apply it to a situation, or use it to analyse or evaluate something. In questions worth more marks, you might need to do a combination of these.

Extended Writing Questions

1) Extended writing questions are worth a whopping six marks — they're marked with an asterisk (*).

2) To answer these questions, as well as showing and applying your PE knowledge, you may need to weigh up the advantages and disadvantages of something, or analyse how or why something happens.

3) At the end of your answer, you might need to write a conclusion where you make a judgement.

You will also be assessed on 'how well you write your answer', so make sure you do these things:

• Organise your answer — jot down what you want to cover in a quick plan before you start writing it. That way you can structure your answer well, and cover all the points you need to in a logical way.

• Answer the question being asked — focus on the topic rather than waffling.

• Write in full sentences and use the correct spelling, grammar and punctuation.

• Use the correct PE vocabulary.

Answering Exam Questions

You get Marks for Meeting Different Assessment Objectives

1) Assessment objectives (AOs) are the things you need to do to get marks in the exams.

2) In each paper, you'll be tested on three AOs:

Assessment objective 1 (AO1) is all about demonstrating knowledge and understanding of a topic.

1) Questions that test AO1 usually ask you to state, define, describe or identify something.

2) They could also get you to label a diagram or complete a table or sentence.

Assessment objective 2 (AO2) is about applying knowledge and understanding of a topic to a context.

1) Questions that assess AO2 might ask you to explain why or how something happens.

2) You'll sometimes need to give examples to back up your points.

Assessment objective 3 (AO3) is about analysing and evaluating.

1) Questions that test AO3 often start with words like analyse, evaluate, assess, discuss or justify.

2) Analysing just means breaking something down into parts or stages to explain it. This can include analysing data to explain what it shows.

3) To evaluate, assess or discuss something, you will need to weigh up its advantages and disadvantages in the context given in the question.

4) Justifying something means giving reasons why it's sensible.

---

3) A lot of questions will test more than one assessment objective — for example, if a question tells you to evaluate something (AO3), you'll also need to demonstrate your knowledge of the topic (AO1) and apply it to the situation in the question (AO2).

In the Exams — Read the Questions and Don't Panic

1) Read every question carefully.

2) The number of marks each question is worth is shown next to it in brackets, or at the bottom of the answer lines. This can be a good guide to the number of points you need to make and how long your answer should be.

The number of answer lines given in a question can also be a good guide to how much to write.

3) Make sure your answers are clear and easy to read. If the examiner can't read your handwriting, they won't be able to give you any marks.

4) Don't panic — if you get stuck on a question, just move on to the next one. You can come back to it if you have time at the end.

Have a look at this Example Question and Answer

1) This example exam answer will show you how marks are awarded for the things you write:

---

15 **Figure 1** shows a performer taking part in archery.
Assess the importance of agility to the archer.

Figure 1

AO1 → *Agility is the ability to change body position or direction quickly and with control.*

AO2 → *Archers need to keep their body in a still, steady position so that they can aim accurately at the target.*

Therefore, agility is not an important component of fitness for an archer. ← AO3

[3]

---

2) This answer gets one mark for each assessment objective it meets.

3) It meets AO1 by defining agility, AO2 by explaining what impact agility has on an archer, and AO3 by evaluating the importance of agility for the archer.

Answers

A note about answers and marks
The answers and mark schemes given here should be used mainly for guidance, as there may be many different correct answers to each question — don't panic if your answers are a bit different.

Section One — Anatomy and Physiology Part 1

Page 1 — The Skeletal System

Q1 E.g. Bones store minerals like calcium and phosphorus, which help maintain bone strength *[1 mark]*. Strong bones prevent the leg/foot bones from breaking when stress is placed on them when landing after leaping to intercept a pass in netball *[1 mark]*.

You could say that these minerals also enable muscle contractions, which allow someone taking part in physical activity to perform the necessary sports movements.

Page 2 — The Skeletal System

Q1 Fibula *[1 mark]* and tibia *[1 mark]*

Q2 C Ulna *[1 mark]*

Page 3 — The Skeletal System

Q1 Ball and socket *[1 mark]*

Q2 Cartilage covers the ends of bones that meet at joints acting as a cushion between them *[1 mark]*. This allows a performer to use their joints for movement without damage to the bones as they rub against each other *[1 mark]*.

Page 4 — The Skeletal System

Q1 E.g. During a netball pass, flexion at the elbow occurs in order to bring the ball backwards towards the player *[1 mark]*. Next, extension at the elbow occurs, straightening the arm and propelling the ball forward towards the target *[1 mark]*.

Page 5 — The Muscular System

Q1 Biceps *[1 mark]* and triceps *[1 mark]*

Q2 In the calf/lower leg *[1 mark]*

Page 6 — The Muscular System

Q1 The quadriceps *[1 mark]*

When kicking a football, the quadriceps allow extension at the knee so the lower leg swings forward.

Page 7 — Lever Systems

Q1 E.g.

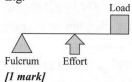

[1 mark]

When performing a squat, the knee is moving from flexion to extension, which uses a third class lever.

Page 8 — Planes and Axes of Movement

Q1 Frontal plane *[1 mark]* and frontal axis *[1 mark]*

A star jump involves abduction of the arms and legs away and towards the body. These movements use the frontal plane and frontal axis.

Section Two — Anatomy and Physiology Part 2

Page 10 — The Cardiovascular System

Q1 E.g. The pulmonary artery carries deoxygenated blood *[1 mark]* to the lungs, where it becomes oxygenated *[1 mark]*.

Page 11 — The Cardiovascular System

Q1 E.g. Capillaries carry blood close to the muscles *[1 mark]*. This allows them to exchange gases and nutrients with the muscles *[1 mark]*.

Page 12 — The Respiratory System

Q1 E.g. Deoxygenated blood becomes oxygenated through gas exchange between the capillaries containing the deoxygenated blood and the alveoli containing oxygen *[1 mark]*. Oxygen diffuses from an area of higher concentration (the alveoli) *[1 mark]* to an area of lower concentration (the deoxygenated blood) *[1 mark]*.

Page 13 — The Respiratory System

Q1 E.g. A 100-metre sprint would be anaerobic exercise because it is a high intensity and short duration event *[1 mark]*. The body's systems would be unable to deliver oxygen quickly enough for the muscles to use aerobic respiration *[1 mark]*, so the muscles would release energy without oxygen *[1 mark]*.

Page 14 — Short-Term Effects of Exercise

Q1 Tidal volume will increase *[1 mark]* so that more oxygen can be delivered to the muscles to allow them to move *[1 mark]*.

Your tidal volume will remain higher than normal after anaerobic exercise until you have repaid the oxygen debt.

Page 15 — Short-Term Effects of Exercise

Q1 During exercise, the **heart rate** *[1 mark]* and stroke volume increase. This leads to an increase in the **cardiac** *[1 mark]* output so more oxygenated **blood** *[1 mark]* is delivered to the muscles.

Q2 This occurs in order to reduce the amount of blood being delivered to the stomach *[1 mark]*. This leaves more blood, and therefore more oxygen, available for the working muscles, where it is used to release the extra energy needed for exercise *[1 mark]*.

Page 16 — Short-Term Effects of Exercise

Q1 a) 63 cm³ *[1 mark]*
b) 141 cm³ *[1 mark]*

Stroke volume increases during exercise and slowly returns to normal after exercise has stopped. So the lowest value in the table must have been recorded before exercise started, and the highest must have been during the high intensity exercise.

Answers

Page 17 — Long-Term Effects of Exercise

Q1 E.g. Muscle hypertrophy means an increase in muscle thickness/ size *[1 mark]*. This would benefit a performer participating in weightlifting because it would increase their strength, meaning they would be able to lift heavier weights *[1 mark]*.

Section Three — Physical Training

Page 19 — Components of Fitness

Q1 E.g. Muscular endurance allows you to repeatedly use muscles without getting tired *[1 mark]*. A long-distance cyclist uses the same leg muscles over a long period of time *[1 mark]*, so muscular endurance is very important in preventing fatigue in the later stages of a race and in helping the cyclist to sprint at the end *[1 mark]*.

Any reasonable application of muscular endurance to a cycling race will get you the third mark here.

Page 20 — Components of Fitness

Q1 E.g. Flexibility will help the swimmer avoid injury, meaning they can train more, which will help them perform better *[1 mark]*. Flexibility will help the swimmer achieve longer/more efficient strokes *[1 mark]*.

Page 21 — Components of Fitness

Q1 E.g. Coordination is the ability to use two or more parts of the body together, efficiently and accurately *[1 mark]*.

Make sure your definition talks about using two or more parts of the body, and you'll get the mark.

A boxer needs good hand-eye coordination to be able to throw a punch accurately *[1 mark]*.

Any example of using two or more body parts together in boxing is okay for the second mark.

Page 22 — Fitness Testing

Q1 Any two from: e.g. To evaluate how successful their training programme is at improving cardiovascular endurance / to get a starting (baseline) level of cardiovascular endurance / so they can compare their cardiovascular endurance with national averages *[1 mark for each]*.

Page 23 — Fitness Testing

Q1 Strength (or 'muscular strength') *[1 mark]*

Page 24 — Fitness Testing

Q1 E.g. The standing jump test measures how far you can jump and the vertical jump test measures how high you can jump *[1 mark]*. A triple jumper needs to jump a long distance, so the standing jump test might be more suitable than the vertical jump test *[1 mark]*.

Page 25 — Principles of Training

Q1 E.g. A rower could train using a rowing machine *[1 mark]*, as this would work the same muscles as they use in their sport *[1 mark]*.

Page 26 — Principles of Training

Q1 E.g. If you don't train frequently enough you will lose the fitness you've gained / Increasing the frequency of training is a way of overloading which increases fitness *[1 mark]*. If you train too frequently, there won't be enough time between training sessions for your body to recover / Training too frequently can lead to injury, which will stop you training and lead to a decrease in fitness *[1 mark]*.

Page 27 — Training Methods

Q1 E.g. Continuous training is good aerobic training *[1 mark]*. This means it is well suited to aerobic endurance activities like marathon running *[1 mark]*. However, continuous training does not improve anaerobic fitness *[1 mark]*, so is not well suited to anaerobic activities like sprinting so its better training for the marathon than the 100 m sprint *[1 mark]*.

Page 28 — Training Methods

Q1 E.g. For strength training, an athlete needs to use a high weight and do a low number of reps *[1 mark]*. They can overload by gradually increasing the weight used *[1 mark]*.

Page 29 — Training Methods

Q1 E.g. Plyometric training increases power *[1 mark]*, which would help the basketball player to jump higher to make interceptions *[1 mark]*.

One mark is for saying plyometric training improves power. One mark is for identifying an action that power helps with in basketball — e.g. jumping, sprinting, shooting.

Page 30 — Preventing Injuries

Q1 This mark scheme gives examples of some points you might have made in your answer. To get full marks you don't need to have written every point, but you do need to include sufficient detail, clearly apply your points to practical situations, draw well-reasoned conclusions, and present your answer in a logical, organised way, using all the right specialist language.

You will get up to two marks for showing knowledge and understanding of a warm-up, for example:

- A warm-up includes light aerobic exercise to gradually increase your pulse rate.
- A warm-up includes stretching the muscles that will be used in the activity.
- A warm-up can include practice actions to prepare the muscles that will be used during the activity.

You will get up to four marks if you also include examples of how the warm-up can help prevent injuries in hockey, for example:

- Practising passing the ball in the warm-up helps prepare the shoulder and arm muscles for passing during the hockey match, so they're warm and less likely to get injured.
- Stretching the leg muscles will help to improve their flexibility, which will help the player to avoid injury when they lunge to reach the ball.
- The light exercise eases the player's body into more intense exercise, which helps them to avoid injury when they need to sprint to outrun other players during the hockey match.

You will get up to six marks if you also evaluate the importance of a warm-up in preventing injury. You can include comparisons with other methods of preventing injury in a hockey match. For example:

- A warm-up is necessary for a hockey player to avoid injury, because stretching and practising actions help prepare the player's muscles for the strenuous actions they'll perform in the match, like lunging for the ball or sprinting.
- However, it is also important to use protective equipment, such as gumshields and shinpads, to prevent injuries.
- In conclusion, a warm-up is vital before a hockey match to help prevent injury. However a warm-up alone is not sufficient to prevent all types of injury, so other measures must also be taken.

[6 marks available in total]

Answers

Page 31 — Preventing Injuries

Q1 E.g. A rugby player can wear a gumshield to prevent injuries to teeth when tackling *[1 mark]*.

Section Four —
Socio-Cultural Influences

Page 33 — Influences on Participation

Q1 E.g. There is less media coverage of women's sports than men's sports / There are fewer female than male sporting role models / There is less sponsorship available for women's sport than men's sport / Gender stereotyping may put some women off participating in sport *[1 mark]*.

Page 34 — Influences on Participation

Q1 E.g. People who work long hours / have family commitments might not have the free time to participate in sport *[1 mark]*.

Page 35 — Influences on Participation

Q1 Any two from: e.g.
Students could be allowed to choose from a range of activities / schools could invest in new facilities, equipment or changing rooms / schools could offer non-competitive options in PE / schools could bring in outside agencies to help with coaching and development *[1 mark for each]*.

Page 36 — Influences on Participation

Q1 **C** Running *[1 mark]*

Page 37 — Commercialisation of Sport

Q1 E.g. Media interest in a sport creates role models *[1 mark]*. This will increase participation by inspiring people watching the sport to participate *[1 mark]*.
Media interest in a sport allows it to reach a much larger audience *[1 mark]*. This will increase participation as more people will be aware of the sport and learn about it, which may encourage them to take it up *[1 mark]*.

With each point, make sure you say enough to get two marks by saying how and why participation is affected.

Page 38 — Commercialisation of Sport

Q1 *This mark scheme gives examples of some points you might have made in your answer. To get full marks you don't need to have written every point, but you do need to include sufficient detail, clearly apply your points to practical situations, draw well-reasoned conclusions, and present your answer in a logical, organised way, using all the right specialist language.*

You will get up to two marks for showing knowledge and understanding of sponsorship in sport, for example:

- Sponsorship would provide funding for the player.
- The company might require the player to fulfil a contract.
- The company might decide to end the sponsorship suddenly.
- The sponsorship might be inappropriate, e.g. a fast-food company.

You will get up to four marks if you also give practical examples of the possible impacts of the sponsorship on the player, for example:

- The sponsorship money could be spent on equipment or high-quality coaching for the player.
- The sponsorship money may allow the player to train full-time.
- The sponsor might demand that the player appears in adverts, or doesn't use competitor products.
- If the deal ended suddenly, the player might struggle with the sudden drop in income, e.g. they might have to drop out of a tournament if they couldn't afford the transportation.
- The player's reputation might suffer if linked to an inappropriate company.

You will get up to six marks if you also evaluate the positive and negative impacts of the sponsorship on the player, for example:

- The sponsorship may help to boost the player's performance through better coaching and equipment, or increased time to train, at least for the duration of the sponsorship.
- It's likely the player will have to allow the sponsor some control over their life in return.
- Depending on the value of the sponsorship, the player might feel the opportunities offered outweigh any loss of control.

Page 39 — Ethical Issues in Sport

Q1 E.g. Deviance is where a participant in a sport breaks the laws of the game *[1 mark]*, whereas gamesmanship only involves bending the rules to gain an advantage, without actually breaking them *[1 mark]*.

Page 40 — Ethical Issues in Sport

Q1 E.g. Beta blockers might benefit an archer because they have a calming effect on shaking hands *[1 mark]*, which will help the archer keep steady as they take aim and shoot *[1 mark]*.

The first mark comes from explaining what the drug does, and the second mark comes from applying that effect to archery.

Section Five —
Sports Psychology

Page 42 — Learning Skills

Q1 E.g. An efficient technique is important for a marathon runner because the more efficient their technique, the less energy they will use *[1 mark]*. Therefore, an efficient technique would help them to run for the duration of a marathon without becoming too tired to continue *[1 mark]*.

You could also say that an efficient running technique would use less time, allowing a runner to complete a marathon more quickly.

Page 43 — Goal Setting

Q1 E.g. This goal does not apply the 'measurable' principle *[1 mark]*. It is not measurable because it does not say how much faster the athlete would like to run *[1 mark]*.

You could also say that the goal doesn't apply the 'specific' principle for the same reason.

Page 44 — Goal Setting and Mental Preparation

Q1 E.g. A football player may imagine the feeling in their muscles when taking the penalty perfectly *[1 mark]*. They could mentally rehearse approaching the ball and the movements involved in kicking it well *[1 mark]*.

Answers

Page 45 — Types of Guidance

Q1 This mark scheme gives examples of some points you might have made in your answer. To get full marks you don't need to have written every point, but you do need to include sufficient detail, clearly apply your points to practical situations, draw well-reasoned conclusions, and present your answer in a logical, organised way, using all the right specialist language.

You will get up to two marks for showing knowledge and understanding of the different types of guidance, for example:

- Verbal guidance includes instructions given in words.
- Verbal guidance involves a coach explaining how to perform a skill.
- Manual guidance involves a coach moving the performer's body through a technique.

You will get up to four marks if you also apply your knowledge of guidance to a beginner in golf, for example:

- Verbal guidance could include the coach telling the learner how to position their legs before swinging the club.
- Manual guidance could include the coach moving the learner's arms through a golf swing.
- Verbal and manual guidance could be used at the same time. For example, the coach could manually position the learner's hands on the club, while explaining how they should be positioned.

You will get up to six marks if you also evaluate which guidance type would be best for use with a beginner golfer. For example:

- Manual guidance can be useful for beginners as it gives them the feel of the correct technique. However, it can lead to the learner relying on it.
- Verbal guidance alone may be confusing for a beginner, as they may be unable to picture how a technique should feel due to their limited experience in golf.
- In conclusion, it would be best to combine verbal and manual guidance to improve a beginner's performance in golf. This would allow the learner to experience how golfing techniques feel while having them explained by the coach, to make sure they understand them.

[6 marks available in total]

Page 46 — Types of Feedback

Q1 E.g. Praise is an example of positive feedback *[1 mark]*. This would teach the beginner that they should continue to use this stance on the snowboard *[1 mark]*, which will encourage/motivate the beginner to keep learning *[1 mark]*.

You could also say that this is extrinsic feedback, which is useful for beginners as they lack the knowledge needed to assess their own performance. It is also knowledge of performance feedback.

Section Six — Health, Fitness and Well-Being

Page 48 — Health, Fitness and Well-Being

Q1 E.g. Regular exercise helps you to maintain a healthy weight, which reduces the likelihood of developing type-2 diabetes *[1 mark]*.

You could also say that regular exercise increases the sensitivity of the body's cells to insulin, which reduces the chances of them becoming insulin-resistant and thus developing type-2 diabetes.

Page 49 — Health, Fitness and Well-Being

Q1 E.g. Partaking in physical activity can increase people's self-esteem and confidence because they feel like they have achieved something, which makes them emotionally healthier *[1 mark]*. Physical activity can be a method of reducing stress as it can act as a distraction from the parts of life which are causing tension *[1 mark]*.

You could also say that physical activity can lead to improvements in the physical appearance of people's bodies, which could lead to them gaining a better self-image and make them more confident.

Page 50 — Sedentary Lifestyles

Q1 E.g. Accelerated bone density loss / increased risk of fractures *[1 mark]*. Obesity *[1 mark]*.

Other answers include emotional/social health problems, such as depression, and poor posture.

Page 51 — Diet and Nutrition

Q1 E.g. Carbohydrates are the body's main source of energy for muscles during physical activity *[1 mark]*.

Page 52 — Diet and Nutrition

Q1 E.g. Proper hydration prevents blood thickening, which would reduce the amount of oxygen reaching the muscles. This would affect the ability of the muscles to work optimally *[1 mark]*. Proper hydration maintains the body's ability to sweat, which prevents overheating and potentially even fainting *[1 mark]*.

Page 53 — Diet and Nutrition

Q1 E.g. Carbohydrates provide easily available energy for your muscles *[1 mark]*. Therefore, they would be more beneficial for a triathlete, as they are exercising for a long time and need a lot of energy *[1 mark]*. For a weightlifter, who needs a diet which can aid in the repair and development of muscle, a diet high in protein would be more beneficial *[1 mark]*.

Section Seven — Using Data

Page 55 — Using Data

Q1 Sarah *[1 mark]*

Sarah had an increase of 6, from 2 tackles to 8. Jenny only increased by 3, from 3 tackles to 6.

Page 56 — Using Data

Q1 B 66 bpm *[1 mark]*

Page 57 — Using Data

Q1 6 minutes *[1 mark]*

Joanna's resting heart rate is 70 bpm, so double her resting heart rate is 140 bpm. Her heart rate is greater than or equal to 140 bpm for 6 minutes, between 14 and 20 minutes.

Glossary

abduction	Movement <u>away</u> from an imaginary <u>centre line</u> through the body.
adduction	Movement <u>towards</u> an imaginary <u>centre line</u> through the body.
aerobic exercise	'With oxygen'. When exercise is <u>not too fast</u> and is <u>steady</u>, the heart can supply all the oxygen that the working muscles need.
agility	The <u>ability</u> to change <u>body position</u> or <u>direction</u> quickly and with control.
alveoli	Small <u>air bags</u> in the <u>lungs</u> where gases are exchanged.
anaerobic exercise	'Without oxygen'. When exercise duration is <u>short</u> and at <u>high intensity</u>, the heart and lungs can't supply blood and oxygen to muscles as fast as the cells need them.
antagonistic muscle action	The action of a pair of muscles that work <u>against each other</u> to bring about movement. As one muscle <u>contracts</u> (the <u>agonist</u>) the other <u>relaxes/lengthens</u> (the <u>antagonist</u>).
axis of rotation	An <u>imaginary line</u> that the body or a body part can <u>move around</u>.
balance	The ability to stay <u>upright</u> and <u>in control</u> of any movement.
balanced diet	The best <u>ratio</u> of <u>nutrients</u> to match your <u>lifestyle</u>.
blood cell	A component of <u>blood</u> made by bone marrow. <u>Red blood cells</u> carry oxygen and carbon dioxide.
blood pressure	How <u>strongly</u> the blood presses against the walls of <u>blood vessels</u>.
blood vessels	Part of the cardiovascular system that <u>transports blood</u> around the body. The three main types are <u>arteries</u>, <u>veins</u> and <u>capillaries</u>.
breathing rate	The <u>number of breaths</u> taken <u>each minute</u>. Also known as <u>respiratory rate</u>.
capillarisation	The <u>increase</u> in the number of <u>capillaries</u> in the muscles and at the alveoli as a long term effect of exercise.
cardiac output	The <u>volume of blood</u> pumped by a ventricle in the heart per minute, calculated by multiplying <u>heart rate</u> by <u>stroke volume</u>.
cardio-respiratory system	The combination of the <u>cardiovascular</u> and <u>respiratory</u> systems working together to get <u>oxygen</u> into the body tissues and <u>carbon dioxide</u> out of them.
cardiovascular endurance/stamina	The ability to <u>continue</u> exercising while getting <u>energy</u> for muscular movement from <u>aerobic</u> exercise.
cardiovascular system	The way in which <u>blood</u> is <u>circulated</u> around the body. The three main parts are the <u>heart</u>, <u>blood</u> and <u>blood vessels</u>.
cartilage	Acts as a <u>cushion</u> between bones to <u>prevent damage</u> during joint <u>movement</u>. Aids joint <u>stability</u>.
circumduction	Movement of a limb, hand or foot in a <u>circular motion</u>, e.g. <u>overarm bowling</u> a cricket ball.
closed skill	A <u>skill</u> that is <u>always</u> performed in the <u>same predictable environment</u>.
commercialisation	The commercialisation of sport means the <u>transformation</u> of sport into something people can make <u>money</u> from, e.g. through <u>sponsorship</u> and the <u>media</u>.
complex skill	A <u>skill</u> which needs lots of <u>concentration</u> or lots of <u>information processing</u> to do.
cool-down	<u>Low-intensity exercise</u> and <u>stretching</u> done <u>after exercise</u> to return your body to a resting state.
coordination	The ability to use <u>two or more</u> parts of the body <u>together</u>, efficiently and accurately.
coronary heart disease	When <u>cholesterol</u> builds up in the <u>arteries</u> around the heart, <u>restricting</u> the flow of <u>blood</u>.

Glossary

data	Information — in words or numbers. Data can be quantitative (numbers) or qualitative (words).
deviance	Behaviour that goes against the moral values or laws of the sport.
diffusion	The process of substances (e.g. oxygen) moving down a concentration gradient from a place where there is a higher concentration to a place where there is a lower concentration.
extension	Opening a joint, e.g. straightening the leg at the knee.
feedback	Information that is given to a performer about their performance. Types include intrinsic (what is felt by the performer), extrinsic (from external sources) and positive or negative.
fitness	The ability to meet the demands of the environment. Fitness can be tested in many ways in order to gain data that can be analysed to find ways of improving it.
FITT	A way of planning fitness programmes to include Frequency, Intensity, Time and Type of training.
fixator	Muscles that assist movement by supporting and stabilising joints and the rest of the body.
flexibility	The amount of movement possible at a joint.
flexion	Closing a joint, e.g. bending the arm at the elbow.
gamesmanship	Gaining an advantage by using tactics that seem unfair, but aren't against the rules.
golden triangle	This shows how sport, the media and sponsorship depend on and influence one another.
guidance	Information or help in developing a skill. Guidance can be visual, verbal, manual or mechanical.
hazards	Things which present a risk that could cause an injury, e.g. slippery floors or broken equipment.
health	A state of complete physical, mental and social well-being and not merely the absence of disease or infirmity.
heart rate	The number of times your heart beats in one minute. It is measured in beats per minute (bpm).
hydration	Having the right amount of water for the body to function properly. If you have too little water, you're dehydrated.
hypertrophy	The thickening or increase in size of muscles as a result of exercise.
joints	Where two or more bones meet. Types of joint include synovial, ball and socket and hinge.
lactic acid	A by-product produced during anaerobic exercise. It makes the muscles feel tired and painful.
lever system	A system that allows the body's muscles to move the bones in the skeleton. A lever system can be first, second or third class, and is made up of a lever arm, effort, fulcrum and load.
ligament	Holds bones together to restrict how much joints can move.
mechanical advantage	When a lever can move a large load with a small amount of effort from the muscles.
the media	Organisations involved in mass communication — e.g. through television, radio, newspapers and the Internet.
mental preparation	Methods of mentally preparing for a performance, including imagery, selective attention, positive thinking and mental rehearsal.
minute ventilation	The volume of air breathed in or out in one minute. It can also be called 'minute volume'.
motor skill	A learned ability to use movement to bring about the result you want.
muscular endurance	The ability to repeatedly use muscles over a long time, without getting tired.

Glossary

obesity	Having a large amount of <u>body fat</u>.
open skill	A <u>skill</u> performed in a <u>changing environment</u>, where a performer has to <u>adapt</u> to external factors.
overload	Working your body <u>harder</u> than it normally would to increase <u>fitness levels</u>.
performance enhancing drugs	Drugs taken by performers in order to <u>improve</u> their performance. Types include <u>stimulants</u>, <u>anabolic steroids</u> and <u>beta blockers</u>.
plane of movement	An imaginary flat <u>surface which runs through the body</u>. They are used to describe the <u>direction</u> of a movement. There are <u>three</u> planes you need to know: <u>sagittal</u>, <u>transverse</u> and <u>frontal</u>.
power	Being able to exert as much <u>strength</u> as possible in the <u>shortest time</u> possible.
principles of training	The <u>four</u> principles to follow in order to <u>optimise</u> your training. They are <u>specificity</u>, <u>progression</u>, <u>overload</u> and <u>reversibility</u>.
progression	A principle of <u>training</u> which involves gradually <u>increasing</u> the <u>level</u> of training.
reaction time	The time taken to <u>move</u> in <u>response</u> to a stimulus.
respiratory muscles	The <u>muscles</u> that help <u>air</u> to move <u>in and out</u> of the <u>lungs</u> (the <u>diaphragm</u> and the <u>intercostals</u>).
reversibility	Any fitness <u>improvement</u> caused by training will gradually be <u>lost</u> when training <u>stops</u>.
rotation	Movement of the body or a body part in a <u>clockwise</u> or <u>anticlockwise</u> motion.
sedentary lifestyle	A lifestyle where there is <u>irregular</u> or <u>no physical activity</u>.
simple skill	A <u>skill</u> which doesn't need much <u>concentration</u> or much <u>information processing</u> to do.
SMART	The <u>principles of goal setting</u>. SMART goals are <u>S</u>pecific, <u>M</u>easurable, <u>A</u>chievable, <u>R</u>ecorded and <u>T</u>imed.
specificity	A principle of <u>training</u> that involves <u>matching</u> training to the <u>activity</u> and to the <u>person</u>.
speed	The <u>rate</u> at which someone is able to <u>move</u>, or to <u>cover distance</u>.
sponsorship	When a <u>company</u> pays to associate their <u>name</u> with some part of a <u>sport</u>, usually to make <u>money</u>.
sportsmanship	Playing <u>fairly</u>, sticking to the <u>rules</u> and being <u>polite</u> and <u>respectful</u> to your opponents.
strength	The maximum amount of <u>force</u> that a <u>muscle</u> or <u>muscle group</u> can apply against a <u>resistance</u>. Types of strength include <u>maximal</u> and <u>explosive</u>.
stroke volume	The <u>amount</u> of blood each <u>ventricle</u> pumps with each <u>contraction</u> or <u>heartbeat</u>.
synovial joint	Where two or more <u>bones</u> are <u>joined together</u> in a joint capsule containing <u>synovial fluid</u>.
tendon	Attaches <u>muscles</u> to <u>bones</u> (or other muscles) to allow bones to <u>move</u> when muscles <u>contract</u>.
tidal volume	The <u>amount of air</u> that is breathed in or out in <u>one breath</u>.
trend	When a graph is generally going <u>up</u> or <u>down</u> over time.
type-2 diabetes	A <u>disease</u> caused by <u>high blood sugar</u> levels due to the body's inability to produce the hormone <u>insulin</u>, or cells becoming <u>resistant</u> to insulin.
warm-up	<u>Preparing</u> your body for <u>exercise</u>. It should involve pulse raising, mobility exercises, stretching, dynamic movements and skill rehearsal.

Index

30 m sprint test 23

A
abdominals 5
abduction 4-6, 8
access (influence on participation) 33-36
achievable (SMART goal setting) 43
adaptations 25, 26
adduction 4-6, 8
advertising 36-38
aerobic capacity 17
aerobic exercise 13, 14, 16, 19, 27, 28
age (influence on participation) 35
agility 21, 23
agonists 6
alveoli 12, 16, 17
anabolic steroids (agents) 40
anaerobic exercise 13, 14, 16, 27-29
antagonists 6
antagonistic muscle action 6
aorta 10
arteries 11
articulating bones 3
atria 10
axes of rotation 8

B
balance 21, 23
balanced diet 51
ball and socket joints 3, 4
bar charts 56
benefits of exercise 48, 49
beta blockers 40
biceps 5, 6
bicuspid valve 10
blood 1, 10-12, 15-17
blood vessels 10, 11, 15
body image 50
bone density 17, 48, 50
bone marrow 1
breathing rate 13, 14, 16, 17
bronchi 12
bronchioles 12

C
capillaries 11, 12, 16, 17
capillarisation 17
carbohydrates 51, 53
carbon dioxide 10-12, 14-16
cardiac output 11, 15-17
cardiovascular endurance 19, 22, 27-29
cardiovascular system 10, 11, 15, 16, 50
carpals 2
cartilage 3
cholesterol 48, 50
circuit training 28
circumduction 4, 5
classifying skills 42
clavicle 2
closed skill 42
commercialisation of sport 37, 38
complex skill 42
components of fitness 19-25, 48

concentration 44
concentration gradient 12, 16
confidence 49
connective tissues 3
continuous training 27
continuum 42
cool-down 30
Cooper 12-minute run/walk test 22
coordination 21, 24
coronary heart disease (CHD) 48, 50
cranium 2
cultural beliefs (influence on participation) 33

D
data 16, 22, 36, 44, 50, 55-57
dehydration 52
delayed onset of muscle soreness 30
deltoids 5
deoxygenated blood 10-12
deviance 39
diabetes 48, 50
diaphragm 12, 17
diet 51-53
difficulty continuum 42
diffusion 12, 16
disability (influence on participation) 34
disposable income (influence on participation) 34
double-circulatory system 10
drugs 39, 40
dynamic movements 30
dynamic stretching 30

E
education (influence on participation) 35
elbow 3, 4, 6
emotional health 48-50
emotional well-being 48-50
energy intake and usage 53
environment (influence on participation) 35
environmental continuum 42
ethical issues 39, 40
ethnicity (influence on participation) 33
exchange of gases 11, 12, 16
explosive strength 19, 29
extension 4-8
external intercostal muscles 12, 17
extrinsic feedback 46

F
family (influence on participation) 34
fartlek training 27
fats 51, 53
feedback 46
femur 2
fibre 53
fibula 2
first class levers 7
fitness 48
  components of 19-22, 48
  testing 22-24

FITT 26
fixators 6
flexibility 20, 24
flexion 4-8
fouls 39
fractures 48
friendship 49
frontal axis 8
frontal plane 8

G
gamesmanship 39
gas exchange 11, 12, 16
gastrocnemius 5
gender (influence on participation) 33
globalisation of sport 37
gluteals 5
goal setting 43, 44
golden triangle 37
graphs 16, 36, 44, 50, 55-57
grip strength dynamometer test 23
guidance 45

H
haemoglobin 11
hamstrings 5
hazards 31
health 48-51
heart 10, 11, 15-17, 48, 50
heart rate 11, 15-17
high blood pressure 48, 50
high-intensity interval training (HIIT) 29
hinge joints 3, 4
hip 3, 4, 6
humerus 2
hydration 52, 53
hypertension 48, 50
hypertrophy 17

I
Illinois agility run test 23
imagery 44
improving participation 36
influences on participation 33-36
injuries 31, 48, 50
intercostal muscles 12, 17
interval training 27
intrinsic feedback 46

J
joint capsule 3
joints 3, 4

K
knee 3, 4, 6
knowledge of performance 46
knowledge of results 46

L
lactic acid 13, 14
latissimus dorsi 5
lever systems 7
ligaments 3
loneliness 49

Index